CRITICAL CONDITIONING

Revised Edition

by
Kathryn Stout, B.S.Ed., M.Ed.

Teach or Tutor Grades K - 8

Critical Thinking
Reading Comprehension Skills
Propaganda Techniques
Literary Elements
Study skills

A Reference for Grades 9-12

A DESIGN-A-STUDY BOOK

OTHER TITLES BY KATHRYN STOUT
Comprehensive Composition
Guides to History Plus
Maximum Math
The Maya
Natural Speller
Science Scope
Teaching Tips and Techniques

Audiocassettes
Developing Attitudes and Habits: What's Important and When
A Chronological Unit Approach to History
How To Teach Composition
Make It Easy on Yourself
Math That Makes Sense
Strategies for Teaching and Learning Spelling
Teaching English: What's Essential?
Teaching Kids to Think
Teaching Reading, Spelling, & Critical Thinking
Teaching Tips That Really Work

Current listings and prices available from Design-A-Study at
Web Site: http://www.designastudy.com/
E-mail: kathryn@designastudy.com
Phone/Fax: (302) 998-3889
or write to the address below.

Published by Design-A-Study
408 Victoria Avenue
Wilmington, DE 19804-2124

Cover Design by Ted Karwowski and Richard B. Stout
Photograph of author by Karl Richeson

ISBN 1-891975-02-1

Library of Congress Catalog Card Number 98-093857

WHAT IS CRITICAL CONDITIONING?

Children must be trained (conditioned) to think critically. This guide helps parents, tutors, and teachers incorporate thinking skills into every aspect of comprehension.

⟹ Read aloud to young children using an approach that directs their thinking, conditioning them to eventually read this way on their own. *(Refer to pages 13-18.)*

⟹ Teach older children to use this method in order to read for insight. *(Refer to pages 13-18.)*

⟹ Develop language skills that enhance the ability to think beyond the literal level. *(Refer to pages 19-48.)*

⟹ Provide insights that help children learn to analyze fiction and nonfiction. *(Refer to pages 39-65.)*

⟹ Do all of the above while meeting standard reading comprehension objectives. *(Refer to pages 76-88.)*

TABLE OF CONTENTS

READING COMPREHENSION SKILLS

Students cannot analyze something they don't first understand on a literal level. Therefore, basic skills continue to be developed at all ages as students listen to and read longer and more complex fiction and nonfiction selections.

☑ Hear language: listen to a variety of styles and types of fiction, nonfiction, and poetry read fluently and with expression that indicates emotion or mood.

☑ Develop the ability to read fluently and with expression, indicating an understanding of what is being read.

☑ Develop the ability to present ideas to a group: use specific vocabulary appropriate to the audience and topic, use visual aids, speak fluently and with appropriate gestures, and make eye contact with the audience.

☑ Follow oral and written directions.

☑ Develop vocabulary, including specific words to describe size, shape, texture, taste, smell, location, people, places, things, emotions, moods, actions, etc.

☑ Develop an understanding of imagery produced through the use of vivid description and figurative language. Students should be able to explain both the literal and non-literal meanings of idioms, similes, metaphors, etc.

☑ Learn phonic skills, meanings of affixes and homophones and recognize multiple meanings of words in order to understand what is heard and read. (Phonic skills are aided by the ability to differentiate sounds, repeat sounds, and identify and create rhyming words and patterns.)

☑ Use clues from pictures, diagrams, titles, headings, and context in order to understand meaning.

☑ Develop the habit of using a dictionary, glossary, or thesaurus in order to find out the meaning of a word. (The ability to alphabetize is necessary to do this efficiently.)

☑ Learn to read information from charts, graphs, diagrams, maps, and globes.

☑ Locate books in a library using the card catalog (or computer), including reference books.

☑ Find and use information in a variety of reference materials, including an atlas, dictionary, encyclopedia, globe, newspaper, telephone directory, and thesaurus.

☑ Locate information quickly: skim or scan material, use the table of contents, index, and/or glossary.

☑ Adjust reading rate to suit the purpose—skim, scan, or survey to find information or study to pass judgment on the selection.

☑ Indicate recall of what was read or heard by restating orally or in writing information or story events in a logical order.

☑ Identify elements in stories and in plays by naming characters (including the narrator, if applicable), describing the setting (and scene) and plot, and restating the main idea.

☑ After reading a selection, answer questions by finding specific information within the piece.

Critical thinking skills begin with simple inferences. Ultimately, the goal is to apply ideas learned to one's own life. Those ideas, however, should not merely be the result of an emotional response, but, rather, the result of applying analytical skills to determine the reliability and usefulness of the information.

☑ Set a purpose for listening and reading.

☑ Make inferences (conclusions based on what is implied, not stated) in order to comprehend meaning.

☑ Identify the author's purpose: to entertain, inform, or persuade (or a combination of all three).

☑ Relate previous experience to what is heard or read.

☑ Differentiate between fact and fantasy, fact and opinion, and fiction and nonfiction.

☑ Identify cause and effect relationships.

☑ Classify information using similarities and differences; compare and contrast information.

☑ Organize important points of selections in a variety of ways: summary, outline, graph.

☑ Take notes and organize them for study.

☑ Recognize a variety of persuasive and propaganda techniques and ways in which they are used.

☑ Evaluate material for propaganda and bias.

☑ Draw conclusions—make generalizations based on the selection read (or heard).

☑ Evaluate sources of information. Express an opinion with support for accepting or rejecting given information.

☑ Identify the type of fiction based on characteristics observed within the selection heard or read.

☑ Make reasonable predictions, and confirm or revise predictions during reading.

☑ Indicate comprehension of the main idea of a selection by explaining it succinctly.

☑ Identify the point of view of the story (first or third person).

☑ Infer emotions or mood of a character.

☑ Infer personality traits of characters, locating evidence within the selection for support.

☑ Describe the development of a character in a fictional work.

☑ Infer the setting in a story (if not specified).

☑ Analyze the plot by describing who acted, what action(s) was taken, and the result(s) of that action(s).

☑ Offer other reasonable conclusions (solutions) to a story.

☑ Explain how the author's choice of vocabulary contributes to a story.

☑ Identify the tone of a poem or story, explaining how it was achieved by referring to various uses of language, including archaic, formal and/or informal and dialect, figures of speech, and any relevant story elements (e.g., character, setting, and plot devices).

TEACH CHILDREN TO THINK CRITICALLY

 The information in this guide can be used informally by parents to encourage their children to think. Discuss books, stories, and articles read by the children or read to them. Also discuss movies, TV programs and commercials. By example, they will learn to look beyond the surface.

Teachers, tutors, and parents should become familiar with the terms in this guide in order to introduce them informally through discussion or activities that provide a meaningful context. Practice can, and should be, applied to content in any subject. The students' focus should be on gaining understanding of anything read or heard, not on memorizing definitions. The students will then recognize that the concept or skill has practical, not merely academic, value.

- Allow students to investigate topics of personal interest. Help them become efficient in using reference skills to find information, and direct them in evaluating whether each resource is usable for their situation *(page 64)*:

    ➡ Who is the author and does he have any expertise in the field?

    ➡ What is the copyright or date of revision?

    ➡ Can this information be considered relevant, or should it be discarded as out of date?

    Developing this as a habit will help them in their selection of books for personal use.

- Encourage students to use references in response to need: a telephone directory to find someone's phone number or address, a dictionary or thesaurus to choose the best word in a composition, maps to find their way around a shopping mall, and so on.

- Students often find analysis difficult, preferring to read for answers to complete worksheets. Allow students to express opinions and attempt to

look beyond factual info. into analysis

prove their points even if it disagrees with an author or teacher. Any student that has a valid point will be encouraged to continue analyzing and contributing to discussions. If a student's point is weak, the teacher can provide necessary feedback to direct his thinking and serve as a model to help him develop both the skill and habit of evaluation.

➡ After watching a movie, discuss its merits based on the elements of literature, encouraging the students to do the same.

➡ Instead of having students simply identify examples of exaggeration, have them discuss whether it is being used for effect (hyperbole, irony), or if it is an unethical stretch of the truth used in an attempt to persuade the reader to a particular point of view. This should become a habit applied to even casual personal reading—magazines, newspapers, advertisements.

● Identify propaganda techniques used in television commercials and encourage the students to do the same.

question the bias of the author

● Examine newspaper articles for bias, identifying examples of opinions given in accounts that should be entirely objective. Older students can then be given articles to read and examine, and an opportunity to offer their opinion.

 Any areas of comprehension that appear difficult for a child can be targeted for extra practice using workbooks or software at the appropriate skill level. The child should practice until it makes sense—until he's mastered that skill at that level. Mastery, not completion of materials, should be the goal.

 The checklist in the back of this guide may be used to keep a record of practice, providing an easy reference for teacher planning. A few areas may be targeted for a short period of time, rather than attempting to cover all skills continuously.

HIGH SCHOOL

High school students should analyze plays and poems—including examples of satire—as well as other types of literature. Study guides from *Monarch Notes*, *Cliff's Notes* and *Barron's Notes* contain chapter summaries, commentaries, and background notes which can be used by the teacher as an aid in directing discussions beyond simple summaries to include customs, history, character motivation, themes, imagery, symbolism, etc.

READING INDEPENDENTLY

Reading aloud enriches children of all ages. As they are inspired to choose books to read on their own, it is important that their enthusiasm be met with success. Teach them to use the simple procedure below to determine whether or not they will be able to read their selection. If it proves to be too difficult, assuage their disappointment by offering to read that book aloud and encouraging them to try another.

FIVE-FINGER GUIDE

1. Open the book to any page.

2. Begin reading.

3. Bend one finger down for each word that cannot be pronounced or is not understood.

4. The book will be too difficult if five fingers are down by the end of one page.

A NOTE TO PARENTS

The level of materials used to teach reading indicate the child's instructional level. Books used for past instruction—those he can now read without help—indicate his independent reading level. When selecting books that list age or grade level, use your child's independent reading level as your frame of reference.

Books are available with content of interest to the actual age of students from nine to eighteen, but with a reading level of grade one, two, three, or four. These may be labeled as high interest and/or low readability books in the local library.

HOW TO READ CRITICALLY

 Have a purpose for reading so that you are reading for meaning.

That is, think of questions and read for answers.

 Question the reasonableness of what you are reading.

Think: How does it compare with what you already know?

What meanings are implied (not simply stated)?

What conclusions can you reach?

 Accept or reject new ideas based on what you already know.

Think: Are the author's points valid?

If you decide that they are, add that information to what you already know, or change your opinion, giving up any ideas you had that no longer seem valid.

 Teach this method informally to young children by implementing the suggestions that follow as you read stories aloud.

<u>Skills Developed By Reading Critically:</u>

- ❑ Set a purpose for listening and reading. (Grades K-8)
- ❑ Make reasonable predictions and confirm or revise predictions during reading. (Grades K-8)
- ❑ Make inferences in order to comprehend meaning. (Grades K-8)
- ❑ Draw conclusions—make generalizations based on reading (or listening). (Grades 1-8)
- ❑ Make up a reasonable conclusion to a story. (Grades 3-8)
- ❑ Classify information according to similarities and differences. (Grades 3-8)
- ❑ Evaluate information and provide evidence to support your opinion. (Grades 4-8)
- ❑ Recognize a variety of persuasive techniques and ways in which they are used. (Grades 5-8)
- ❑ Evaluate material for propaganda and bias. (Grades 5-8)

Think ahead to what might happen
Ask why?
Is author qualified
Do you like a character + why
Did you get enough info.

1

DECLARING A PURPOSE*

1. Look at the selection and think of a question. Use the title, pictures, the type of book, any knowledge you have of the author, summaries or questions on the book jacket, or anything else to help you decide what to look for.

☞ Each reader should choose his own purpose. Suggestions may be offered, but by choosing his own question the reader will be encouraged to think rather than look for a right answer. He may begin by just wondering what the book will be about.

2. After choosing a question, predict what you think the answer will be. Again, refer to the title, pictures, the type of book, knowledge of the author, summaries with questions on the book jacket, and any of your own past experiences or other stories you've read.

3. If after reading a few sentences, it is obvious that the purpose question won't be answered, simply think of another question.

4. Once you find the answer, think of another question and make another prediction, then continue reading. Continue with this pattern throughout the selection.

☞ It is not important to be right, only to be reasonable when you predict what might happen, or what answers you will find. As you read, new information may cause you to change your prediction. You are like a detective solving a case and you should be able to give evidence if you think your prediction is right.

**Methods based on the DRTA approach by Dr. Russell Stauffer.*

Teaching Students to Declare a Purpose

Children in grades K - 3 will need guidance establishing a habit of predicting, reading, and proving a prediction, but this approach should continue through all age-levels.

By guiding students through the procedure, they will eventually learn to automatically approach a selection by thinking, hypothesizing, looking for proof, weighing alternatives, and examining evidence. Skimming and scanning skills will be developed as a student rereads to prove his point.

Questions may be part of a group discussion when several students are reading the same selection, or used by the teacher to direct an individual's thinking. The teacher should ask a question calling for a prediction. Once the student responds, have him explain why he thinks his prediction will be right. After he has read a portion (or listened to you read) as if the prediction was right or wrong and why.

SAMPLE

1. Direct students attention to the cover illustration (if any) and title of the story and then ask:

    "What do you think the story [or article] will be about? What do you think will happen?"

    If reading a picture book to young children direct them to look at the next few pictures after they have responded and ask them:

    "Do you need to change your guess or not? Could your first idea be right? If not, try a new idea."

2. Direct students to read (or read aloud to them) until they discover that their guess is correct or until they have enough new information to think they may be wrong. Now that they have more information, direct them to make another prediction about what will happen next.

    For example, if a problem has been introduced, ask how they think it will be solved and why.

3. Direct students' attention to pictures. Ask them to guess who the characters are (relationships—father/son, teacher/student, friends, etc., unless they have already read enough information to guess a name), what they are doing and/or may be saying. Have them read further and then discuss any changes to their thinking.

SAMPLE PURPOSE QUESTIONS

Encourage students to make predictions and look for proof, or, based on new information, make a new prediction continuously throughout a story. This can be accomplished in a fairly short time by participating in the procedure with them regularly, (reading aloud to the young and silently along with older students) and then only occasionally to see if it has become a habit. Use any of the following sample purpose questions to direct their thinking.

1. What kind of person is the main character?

2. Why does _____ live _____ ? *(The snail in a shell, the three bears in the woods, the giant above the clouds, etc.)*

3. How does _____ work? What does it do? *(Stories or picture books of machines: cars, planes, trains, trucks, etc.)*

4. Why does that person look _____ *(sad, mad, puzzled, etc.)* in the picture?

5. How is _____ made?

6. Why does it _____ *(rain? snow? get hot? get dark?)*

7. Why do _____ _____ ? *(birds fly? leaves change color?)*

8. Why is _____ important enough to have a book written about him/her? What special thing did he/she do? Why did he do it? Did he have an easy life?

9. How does the _____ *(boy, girl, man, woman, baby, dog, cat, etc.)* in the picture feel and why?

10. Why is the story called *(title)*?

In early grades especially, a child should discuss his ideas based on questions like those listed below. This allows the teacher to help in shaping the skills used in reasoning: classifying, inferring information, comparing and contrasting, making generalizations, noticing details, drawing conclusions, and weighing alternatives.

1. Keep on asking questions and looking for answers while you read.

2. Look for proof that your predictions are right, or for reasons to change them.

3. Try to figure out any new words by looking for clues—pictures, how it's used in the sentence (context), or a description in the paragraph. If you're still not sure, look up the word in a dictionary.

4. Think about how the book makes you feel, and why.

    If the book is **fiction** (not true):

    - Does it make you laugh? Why? Because of silly situations? Because of the way characters dress or talk? Or because of the outrageous way they handle a problem?

    - Does it make you sad? Why? Do the words make a sad picture in your mind? Do you think something sad is going to happen because of what you've already read or because of a picture? Or, do you feel as if you are experiencing the same feelings as the character as you read? (Note: this is called *empathy* and can be introduced into their literature vocabulary at age 8 or older.) Does he find out how to handle the problem? Do you think that would work for you?

    - Do you like the main character? Because he is like you? Because you want to be like him? Because he is different and you would like to be friends with him?

If the book is **nonfiction** (true):

- Are you eager to read more? Is it because the ideas are so interesting? Because there are great pictures?

- Do you feel satisfied that you learned enough, or does it seem like something was left out because you have questions that weren't answered?

- If the book is an autobiography or biography, do you like the main character? Why? Because he is like you? Because you want to be like him? Because he is different and you would like to be friends with him?

JUDGING WHAT YOU READ

1. Are you content with the proof the author gives for his points, or did you have to assume something that isn't proven?

2. Have you read anything inconsistent with what you already know?
   Are these inconsistencies allowed because of the type of story they are in?
   (E.g.: tall tale, fantasy, fairy tale.)

3. If not, does the author give you enough proof to change your mind, or do you think the author is wrong? Think of reasons to prove your position. What are the sources of the author? What are your sources? When was the book written? Has new evidence been proven since?

4. Does the action of the main character make sense according to everything the author has told you? Would it make sense for you to do the same thing?

5. What is the author trying to say? (main idea, theme)
   Do you agree? Why or why not?

 Remember to use reason, not emotion, to support your opinion.

BUILDING THE FOUNDATION

AGES 3 - 7

PROVIDE EXPERIENCES TO DEVELOP LANGUAGE SKILLS.

1. Read aloud frequently and with expression. Use changes in the tone of your voice to suggest mood. Never assume everything said is understood; instead, offer explanations. Encourage the enjoyment of words and meanings.

2. Read or tell stories and poems that include repeated phrases (patterns).

3. Have children recite stories or poems or sing songs with repeated phrases.

4. Read fairy tales, tall tales, fables and legends as well as poems, short stories, and nonfiction.

5. Provide opportunities for children to attend plays and puppet shows.

6. Encourage children to dramatize stories they have heard. Keep a box of dress-up clothes handy.

7. Have students act out stories with puppets. A puppet can be made quickly by cutting out a character's shape and having the child draw in features, color it and tape it to the top of a ruler.

8. Encourage children to retell stories or experiences in chronological order.

9. Encourage children to relate literature to their own lives:
    Have they seen any of the things in the story?
    How would they feel in that situation?
    What would they do if they were that character?

10. Ask questions that encourage comparisons and have children discuss advantages and disadvantages.

11. Point to illustrations and ask about the mood or emotion expressed.

12. Encourage children to look at appropriate illustrations to find clues about what is happening.

13. Ask questions about the story or pictures: who, what, when, and where. (For young children, when may simply be day or night.)
    Where does the story take place? *(This introduces the idea of setting.)*
    Who is it about?
    What do you think will happen? *(This is a prediction—refer to page 13.)*
    What would you do?
    What happens?

14. When children are very young, point out the lesson or theme (main point) in stories from one to five pages in length. As they are able, ask what they think is the author's lesson. Often this is stated and can be reread to increase their awareness of theme.

15. Point out and explain interesting expressions, phrases, or word choices. Use a large vocabulary around children and encourage their attempts at imitation.

16. Point out expressions or use of imagery and ask about the meaning or mood expressed.

17. Explain expressions and point out figures of speech during daily conversations as well as in literature. Reading young children stories about Amelia Bedilia is an entertaining way to expose children to idioms. She is a maid who takes each order literally. When told to "dress the chicken for dinner," for example, she places the raw bird in a serving dish and adds booties and ribbons.

18. While reading a story, ask about elements that may be fact and those that must be fantasy. Children's stories often involve talking animals. The use of personification gives the animals all the real emotions and behaviors of people, but the idea that animals can talk and act like people is fantasy. At this age the purpose is to help children distinguish between what is real and what is imaginary—what is possible or plausible, and what is not.

19. When reading a story aloud, ask children to describe the mood of a character. (How does he feel? How do you know?) Point out clues in any illustrations as well as by repeating descriptive words or phrases.

20. When reading short (two to six page) stories, point out changes in a character's mood or emotions and the causes of any changes. Ask children to describe how the character felt in one situation at the beginning as opposed to another situation by the middle or end, reviewing what happened in between. As a child is able, ask him to describe how the character felt at the beginning and at later points and why.

21. Point out the problem in a story and ask what they think should be done to solve it before reading the actual solution. (If they have a reasonable solution be sure to express your approval. Continue by saying "Let's see how the author decided to solve the problem" in order to assure them that you were not asking for "right predictions" only reasonable ones.)

22. Read stories and poems with rhyme and meter in order to help children develop an ear for language—its rhythm and flow.

23. Have children make up a new ending or an additional stanza for a poem they have just heard.

24. Have children create a poem with the same rhythm as one just heard.

25. Have children memorize and recite poems.

26. Have children illustrate a story or poem they have heard or created.

27. Read riddles and jokes that are humorous because of the multiple meanings of many words.

28. Provide opportunities for children to move to music as well as sing along.

29. Have children identify sounds as same or different.

30. Provide common sounds for children to identify by listening only: alarm clock, door bell, knock at door, door closing or slamming, key turning in a lock, lawn mower, running water, a person whistling, a steam kettle

whistling, animal sounds (dog barking, cat mewing or purring, bird singing), cars, trucks, and various instruments.

31. Ask children to repeat patterns of sound by clapping, using an instrument, or singing.

32. Have children identify rhyming words and pictures of words that rhyme.

33. Have children make up rhyming words.

34. Play simple action games that allow children to practice sequence and follow oral one- and two-step directions: *Simon Says*, *Follow the Leader*, songs with accompanying movements.

35. Teach children a variety of ways to sort a collection of pictures or objects: by size, shape, texture, color, or use, for example.

36. Give children opportunities to describe:

    • Ask for words to describe tastes, sounds, smells, and sights within their own environment.

    • Give them a picture and ask them to describe the mood, what is happening, what might happen next, or what happened before.

    • After spending time with a friend ask them to describe what they did together, a problem they encountered and its solution, and/or what they enjoyed doing with that friend and why.

37. Write the words dictated by a child as he creates his own story or retells an experience, allowing room on each page for his illustration (by drawing, using stickers or pictures he can cut and paste). Write the title and his name as author on the cover. Add a back and use brass fasteners to secure his book.

38. Choose from among the words he has dictated (#37), write one per index card, and keep these in a box for the student to practice reading and arranging into sentences. This is part of the language experience method that encourages reading by having the student's own words written and read.

39. Encourage young children to make booklets about themselves using drawings, photographs, or cut and paste pictures, dictating descriptive sentences or captions for each. Illustrations may include self-portraits, family portraits, homes, pets, and favorites (colors, songs, foods, activities, places).

40. Have students make vocabulary booklets. They can trace or write the word and draw or cut and paste illustrations for each word. Include color words, meaningful places, people, and objects.

41. Have students help make a booklet or poster of samples of fabric. Draw a shape on the fabric to be used as the line on which they are to cut. Write the name of the fabric on handwriting paper for them to trace. Cut out the label and mount both in a booklet or on a poster. Include velvet, corduroy, linen, cotton, calico prints, plaid patterns, and any other fabrics or designs mentioned in stories.

42. Provide practice with sequencing skills that aid in recalling and organizing information. Direct children to:

     ▪ Tell, dictate, or write directions for making something or doing something that they can do well. Be sure instructions are in the right order so that someone else can do what they instruct.

     ▪ Arrange pictures provided by the teacher in a logical sequence.
       Note to the teacher: Use sets of three to five pictures that illustrate familiar, daily life patterns—seed, seedling, full-grown plant; child setting the table, family eating, children clearing table, dishes being washed. Also use pictures that illustrate events in a story. (Pictures for both daily life and story sequences are available commercially.)

     ▪ Arrange sentences provided by the teacher to form a logical paragraph.
       Note to the teacher: Cut out or copy three- to six-step directions, removing any numerals that might indicate order. Paragraphs from books may also be cut into individual sentences and used.

QUESTIONS TO ENCOURAGE THINKING

A story can touch one reader on a deeper level than another person reading those same words. It is this reaction that causes the reader to come away from the story with a lesson learned, determination to do or be something, or encouragement to continue on. Always allow such sincere responses to be expressed freely and completely. The discussion questions are merely guides—examples to trigger thoughts about what was read in order to help the reader gain insight.

Ideally, discussions should lead the reader into an evaluation of values and give him ideas about how to live up to the values he recognizes as worthwhile. For example, when the poor but kind hero wins over evil, the reader is encouraged to continue being kind even when he feels "picked on." When a character achieves fame ruthlessly and finds himself without friends, the reader recognizes that the end does not justify the means, nor does this philosophy lead to happiness.

Although a student will react emotionally to a work, he isn't always able to recognize why. By directing a student's thinking, he can begin to articulate the why and consciously gain insight from a selection that he can then relate to his own life.

- ◆ **Structure questions so that students must analyze rather than report, evaluate rather than recall. Remember that you are teaching them how to gain insight about life in what they read.**

- ◆ **Ask <u>why</u> more often then who, what, when, where, or how.**

- ◆ **Ask questions narrow enough to require specific, not vague, support.**

- ◆ **Act as a model by offering your own opinions with support.**

- ◆ **Limit the number of questions per selection rather than trying to cover every skill with each lesson, otherwise students may lose interest in both reading and thinking.**

Questions may be used for discussion or as topics for compositions.

Types of Questions

Compare   Explain how things are alike and different.
(Compare/Contrast)

Explain   Make clear. This often requires pointing out cause and effect.

Evaluate   Give advantages and disadvantages (limitations)—good points and bad.

Summarize   Briefly give main points.

          Refer to definitions and explanations in *Comprehending Fiction* (page 49) to enhance discussions.

 **GENERAL FICTION**

Skill: Identify the type of fiction based on characteristics observed within the selection heard or read. *(Refer to pages 50 - 53 for definitions.)*

1.   What kind of fiction is this story? (Tall tale, fairy tale, realistic fiction, historical fiction, mystery, science fiction, etc.)

2.   Were the problems solved in ways acceptable to this type of fiction? For example, if it was a fairy tale there might be magic involved, a tall tale might contain funny and ridiculous exaggeration, but neither of these would be acceptable elements in realistic fiction.

Skill: Develop an understanding of imagery produced through the use of vivid description and figurative language. Students should be able to explain both the literal and non-literal meanings of idioms, similes, metaphors, etc.

3.   Find a figure of speech (simile, metaphor, etc.) that you especially liked. What does it mean? Why do you think the author chose this approach to creating a mental picture instead of a longer explanation?

Skill: Relate previous experiences and learning to the selection.

4.   What do you like best about the story, the plot, the characters, or the theme? Why?

5.   Which incident did you like best in the story? Why?

Skill: Analyze the plot by describing who acted, what action(s) was taken, and the result(s) of that action.

Skill: Offer other reasonable conclusions to a story.

6.   What is the problem (conflict) in the story? How is it resolved? Do you think that was a good way to solve the problem? Why or why not? What other solution would you suggest?

Skill: Relate previous experiences and learning to the selection.

Skill: Infer personality traits of characters, locating evidence within the selection for support.

Skill: Infer emotions or mood of a character.

Skill: Describe the development of a character in fiction.

7.   Choose a character. What is that character like? Find passages to support your opinion. (Examples: lazy, helpful, friendly, reliable, independent, moody, shy, undependable, kind, generous, considerate, selfish, stingy, aggressive, passive.)

8.   Which character did you admire most? Explain. Provide specific examples from the story to support your opinion.

9. Choose a specific character and incident and explain why you think the character acted as he did.

    Skill: Identify the main idea of a selection by explaining it succinctly.

    Skill: Relate previous experiences and learning to the selection.

10. What is the theme (lesson, moral, main idea) of the story?

11. Do you agree or disagree with this lesson or message? Why or why not?

12. Explain the meaning of the title in relation to the story.

13. Why do you think the author chose this title?

14. Look at the way problems were resolved and what lessons were learned by the characters. Based on these things do you think the author has a Christian perspective about life? Give examples from the story to support your opinion.

    Skill: Relate previous experience to what is heard or read.

    Skill: Recognize a variety of persuasive and propaganda techniques and ways in which they are used.

15. If you liked the book, think of your reasons. Then try to "sell" us on the idea that others should read it, too.

16. Pick a scene that especially impressed you (a vivid description, a point you like, or disagree with.) Read it out loud. Tell how it relates to the story and why you chose it.

17. How would your life be different if you lived in this society? Do you think that it would be a better or worse life? Why?

FOLKTALES, MYTHS, LEGENDS

Skill: Compare and contrast information.

1.   Compare folktales from two or more cultures. How are they alike?

   • Do they convey the same values?

   • What is considered good in each culture? Beauty? Strength? Stealing without being caught *(Arabian tales)*? Obedience? Wealth? Kindness?

   • How are problems solved? Magic? Intelligence? Luck?

2.   Compare any folktales to Bible stories or Jewish folktales.
     Notice the value given to wisdom from God.

   • Which values are the same?

   • Which are different?

3.   How do the ideas in the myth compare to the Bible's explanation of creation?

Skill: Infer personality traits of characters, locating evidence within the selection for support.

4.   Are there witches, dragons, or giants in the story?

   • Are they considered good or evil?

   • What is their source of power?

   • What attitude do the people have toward these creatures?

     (E.g., the Chinese think of dragons as good, but dragons in popular fairy tales are considered evil.)

   • Are they feared? Worshipped? How—gladly or in fear?

BIGGER–THAN–LIFE HEROES

Skill: Describe the development of a character in a fictional work.

Skill: Infer emotions or mood of a character.

Skill: Infer personality traits of characters, locating evidence within the selection for support.

1. What are the characteristics of the hero?

2. Does he have power to kill or spare lives? Who gives him that power? Pagan gods? God? The law?

3. Is there a symbol of his power? It may be the instrument he uses to fight—a sword, bow, hammer, etc.

4. Does the hero have a special vehicle? Superior horse? Superior ship? A car with special equipment?

5. Is he kind? This does not mean good, or that all his values are Christian.

6. What motivates the hero? Is he on a special mission? Is it something noble?

Examples of bigger-than-life heroes include Odysseus, Jason, King Arthur, Superman, James Bond. For bigger-than-life heroes, questions 2 - 5 are true. The hero also has a special mission and noble purpose (question #6).

Skill: Compare and contrast information.

7. Look at some heroes in the Bible. Do any have some or all of the qualities of a bigger-than-life hero? What about Samson, for example? Was he kind? What weaknesses lead to his downfall, and what brought him to one final, glorious action? (Samson's hair is the symbol of his power which comes from God's authority, and his superior strength is to be used to kill the enemy of God's people.)

BIOGRAPHIES

Reading biographies provides an enjoyable link between history and/or science and literature. A follow-up discussion in which the teacher directs the students' thinking helps students develop an awareness of the evidence that supports a conclusion.

Skill: Infer personality traits of characters, locating evidence within the selection for support.

Skill: Infer emotions or mood of a character.

Skill: Relate previous experience to what is heard or read.

Skill: Identify the main idea of a selection by explaining it succinctly.

1. Why does the author think this person's life should be shared? Because of something he achieved? Because of ideas or values he believed in?

2. Did the person being written about have a goal or sense of purpose? If so, at what age did he begin working toward that goal (in his youth, middle age, or old age)?

3. Why did he choose that goal? Was he influenced by an encouraging parent? A personal faith? An overwhelming interest in something? A specific experience?

4. What motivated him to work toward it?

5. How did other children react to him when he was a child?
    Did he have many friends or was he looked at as different?

6. How did adults treat him as a child?

7.   What difficulties did he encounter in trying to reach his goal?

8.   How did he overcome difficulties?

9.   How did he handle discouragement?

10. What sacrifices did he make in order to achieve his goal?

11. How did his reaction to difficulties and discouragement, and the choices he made (what he sacrificed) indicate his view of life?

12. If this person did not have a sense of purpose or a goal, look for any event or difficulty that illustrates how he viewed life's obstacles both as a child and as an adult. Is there any difference? If so, what brought about the change in attitude? Is his reaction to problems consistent with his view of life?

     (Examples of views toward life's difficulties: self-pity, helplessness. A change could be a resolve to help others, to persevere rather than feel helpless or defeated. The reason for the change could be the influence or the example of some person, a spiritual change resulting in trust that God has a purpose, or will power and determination—a positive thinking sort of approach.)

13. How were others affected by his life?

14. How would you describe this person? What were his strengths and his weaknesses?   (Think of four or five adjectives.)

     Skill: Evaluate sources of information. Express an opinion with support for accepting or rejecting given information.

15. Older students may find out how information for the biography was acquired and what types of sources were used (interviews, news clippings, diaries, etc.) They could also read two different biographies (or an autobiography and a biography) of the same person to discover how facts can be presented to support the author's own impression or agenda.

 **POETRY**

Skill: Listen to a variety of styles and types of poetry.

Skill: Indicate comprehension of the main idea of a selection by explaining it succinctly.

Skill: Identify the tone of a poem or story, explaining how that was achieved.

Skill: Develop an understanding of imagery produced through the use of vivid description and figurative language. Students should be able to explain both the literal and non-literal meanings of idioms, similes, metaphors, etc.

Skill: Explain how the author's choice of vocabulary contributes to a story.

Skill: Compare and contrast information.

1.   What is the poem about?

2.   What is the main idea?

3.   What is the mood of the poem?

4.   Point out word choices, metaphors, and/or similes that contribute to the creation of that mood.

5.   Find an example of the use of figurative language and explain its meaning in your own words giving emphasis as to why it was an appropriate choice for that particular poem.

6.   Compare and contrast a short narrative poem or ballad (e.g., *Casey Jones* by Siebert and Newton) and a short story. Answer the following questions for each selection:
How many characters are there?
Are characters well-developed or stereotyped?
How many conflicts (problems) are there?

7.   Compare and contrast a narrative poem to a work of fiction that is longer than a short story and answer the same questions listed in #6 above.

ACTIVITIES

Reading comprehension skills are used in every subject area. Additional activities are also available in Design-A-Study books covering other subjects.

LEARNING THE LANGUAGE OF LITERATURE

Students of all ages continue to benefit from listening to literature read aloud. Audio and videocassette recordings of stories can be used as a supplement.

1. Write a word to look like its meaning, such as **f a l** or fall written with colorful letters like autumn leaves. **l**

2. Provide cards with idioms on one set and meanings on another. Students match each meaning to its appropriate idiom.

3. Draw a picture of the idiom as if each word meant exactly what it says.

Examples of idioms:

Follow in his footsteps	*means*	Be the same as
Keep your eyes peeled	*means*	Pay attention
Blow your stack	*means*	Get angry
Take a shot at	*means*	Try
Stole the show	*means*	Received the most positive attention
Stick to your guns	*means*	Don't give in
Put your foot down	*means*	Stand firm
Put your foot in your mouth	*means*	Say something embarrassing
Jump at the chance	*means*	Eager to
Keep your nose to the grindstone --		Work hard
Runs rings around	*means*	Is far superior to
Cry your heart out	*means*	Cry hard
On cloud nine	*means*	Extremely happy
The whole nine yards	*means*	Includes everything being discussed
Hits the nail on the head	*means*	A description that very accurately sums up a situation or person.

4. Listen to tongue twisters, then create some phrases or sentences, beginning each word with the same sound (alliteration).

5. Identify or create phrases using alliteration that relate to a character in a story. *Cautious Katey can't cope.*

6. Identify or create phrases using alliteration that relate to an event in a story. *Slippery snakes slither silently.*

7. Watch for similes and metaphors. List five similes and five metaphors you find in your reading. Illustrate one (or one of your own) from the list. *(Definitions of simile and metaphor are on page 59.)*

8. Read several Psalms. Find examples of metaphors or similes. Explain the meaning. Why you think each creates an image more effectively than a longer explanation.

9. Find or write an example of personification. How does personification effect the mood? Change the mood by writing the description without personification.

10. Read joke books. Explain why each joke is funny.

11. Read riddles. Try writing a riddle.

12. Try writing a riddle using rhyme.

    I'm orange and crunchy and come all bunchy.
    What am I? *(carrot)*

13. Choose a poem you especially enjoy. Write a poem using the same pattern of rhyme and meter.

14. Write a **cinquain** about a character in a story, yourself, or someone you know.

   A cinquain poem has five lines and a pattern, but not a rhyme.
   Line one: one word   Christopher
   Line two: two words   Strong swimmer
   Line three: three words   Writer of stories
   Line four: four words   Master of the Violin
   Line five: one word   Renaissance

15. Choose a story you've enjoyed and list all the words and phrases you can find that the author used instead of the word "said."

16. Create a reference page of words describing personality traits that can serve as an aid when discussing or writing about characters in a story. Use a thesaurus as well as words you read in stories to compose your list.

17. Choose a character in a story. List five adjectives to describe that character. Write a simile for each of the five adjectives.

18. Find an example of a descriptive sentence in a story. Repeat the sentence with only the simple subject and verb, (don't read the descriptive words).
   The author has tried to give you a specific mental picture. Use different descriptive words but the same simple subject and verb to change that image.

19. Write a simple sentence—subject then verb. Now add descriptive words (adjectives, adverbs, similes, and/or metaphors) to make that sentence less vague. (The pencil is on the table. The stubby, yellow pencil with the chewed eraser is on the small wooden table in front of the window.)

20. Choose a proverb or adage and give examples of actions that illustrate its meaning.

   Examples: Honesty is the best policy.
               Do unto others as you would have them do unto you. (Luke 6:31)
               It is better to give than to receive. (Acts 20:35)

21. Maintain a vocabulary notebook, or use index cards and a file box. Use one card for each word. Write the word, its pronunciation, two or three synonyms and an antonym, and a sentence using the word. (Grades 4-8, add its part of speech.) If possible, draw a picture illustrating the word. (Keep index cards in alphabetical order.) Use a dictionary and a thesaurus.

22. Choose three vocabulary cards without looking at the words. Now use all three words in one sentence.

23. Use the dictionary to find out the origins of five of your vocabulary words. (Add this to your card.)

24. Assign a composition that requires using any one or a few figures of speech, and/or writing techniques.

25. Have older students keep a notebook of terms defined in "The Language of Literature" (pages 57-60). As they read, have them either quote an example, or list the book and page number where it can be found. They could also write their own examples.

BUILDING UNDERSTANDING

Sequence

Comprehension begins at the literal level. Basics include identifying details of what was heard or read, and recalling the main points or events in chronological order. The length and complexity of selections should increase in keeping with the student's age and maturity.

1. Act out a story. Older students may dramatize plays, participate in dramatic readings of portions of plays, or turn a short story into a dramatic production.

2. Use puppets to act out a story. Puppets can be made quickly by drawing a character, cutting it out and taping it to the top of a ruler.

3. Write or tell directions for making something or doing something that you do well. Be sure they are in the right order so that someone else can do what you do.

4. Arrange pictures provided by the teacher in a logical sequence.
Note to the teacher: Use sets of 3-5 pictures that illustrate familiar, daily life patterns—seed, seedling, full-grown plant; child setting the table, family eating, children clearing table, dishes being washed. Also use pictures that illustrate events in a story. (Pictures for both daily life and story sequences are available commercially.)

5. Arrange sentences provided by the teacher to form a logical paragraph. (This may be three to six-step directions with no numerals to indicate the correct sequence.) (Grades 3-8)

6. Arrange three to five paragraphs supplied by the teacher in chronological order. (Grades 4-8)

Story Elements, Summaries, and Outlines

Summaries involve describing only the main points or events.

1. The teacher should provide a collection of interesting illustrations. The student should choose a picture, tell what is happening in the picture, then make up reasons why. This provides preparation for creating stories.

2. Make a book jacket for a book you enjoyed. Design a cover that expresses something about the book. Choose colors that reflect the mood of the book.

3. Write a short summary that doesn't give away the ending, but will persuade people to read the book. You can present the problem and then say something like "Find out how—" (or why).

4. Write a book report. The first paragraph should include facts about the book—the title, author, and either the type of book or the general subject. Summarize the book in the next paragraph or two by giving examples of interesting events or other information. The final paragraph can include your opinion and reasons (specific strengths or weaknesses) for that opinion. (Grades 4-8)

5. Write a summary of a selection read using only one to three sentences. (Grades 5-8)

6. Draw an illustration that summarizes the story.

7. Write a title for a short story. The title should not only interest the reader, but relate to the main idea of the story.

8. Given a list of characters and a list of traits, match the personality traits to each character.

9. List the characters in the story. Next to the name of each character list adjectives describing the character's personality as well as his physical appearance.

10. Fill in a book outline made up of the following headings: (Grades 5-8)
Title:
Author:
Setting:
Main characters:
Plot:
Main Idea:
Point of View:
Summary:

11. Choose an idiom. Write a funny story telling how that expression might have begun. Before you write, decide where your story will take place, what will happen, and who will be the first to use the expression.

LEARNING TO ANALYZE

Cause and Effect

1. Provide a cause/effect relationship. Ask the student to identify the cause. Provide a cause/effect relationship. Ask the student to identify the effect. Use a variety of examples, continuing this process. (*Psalms* and *Proverbs* offer several examples. Look for statements that could include If---Then---.) (Grades K-3)

2. Choose an event or situation from the story. What were the circumstances that caused this to happen?

3. Now notice the reaction of the character to the situation, what did he do? Note the action of the character and consequences of that action.

4. Read a nonfiction article that discusses a problem. List causes and effects.

5. Write the effect for any of these causes: an earthquake, a volcano erupting, a hurricane. (Incorporate research skills by having the student track down the necessary information.)

6. Notice that causes are often also the effect of another cause. Start by giving a student a simple statement to pick out the cause and effect before introducing him to this more complicated idea.

Classify, Compare and Contrast

1. Maintain a book list recording book title, author, and type or category of book: E.g., nonfiction, poetry, short story, myth, fable, legend, historical fiction, etc.

2. Choose two characters in a story and tell how they are alike and different.

3. Read stories that take place in different settings: city/country, apartment/house, warm climate/cold climate (and so on). Compare daily life in each setting. (Look at food, clothing, games children play, pets and animal life.) Which setting would you prefer to live in and why?

4. Read stories, legends or folktales from two different cultures. How might these cultures be alike and/or different based on the ideas presented in these selections?

5. Compare the values of the main character with your own. How they are the same and how do they differ?

6. Look for proverbs or adages from other cultures or time periods. Compare them with values taught in the Bible. (Confucius - China, Ben Franklin - early America)

7. Choose an adage (saying) that is not in the Bible and compare it to Bible teachings.

    Examples: Easy come, easy go.
                  You only live once.
                  No good deed goes unpunished.

8. Watch a movie version of a story you have read or listened to. Compare the two versions. Was the same theme expressed in both? Were there any changes to the conflict or its resolution? Were the characters' personalities the same? Do you think the movie version was as good as the book? Why or why not?

9. After reading a story, write about a similar situation in your own life.

10. Choose two reference sources and tell what you could find in both, and what you can only find in one or the other.

Make Inferences and Draw Conclusions

1. If the setting of a story is implied, not stated, tell where and when the story takes place and which clues you used to draw that conclusion.

2. Find an especially descriptive passage that creates a mood, or emotional reaction. Try to create that same mood or reaction in a drawing. (The teacher can select and read a passage for the students.)

3. Find a descriptive passage that uses precise language to give you a picture of a person, place, or thing. Draw a picture according to that description.

4. Choose an emotion (e.g., happy, sad, jealous). Give an example of something someone could do to indicate that mood without using the word you choose. (Consider facial expressions, tone of voice, dialogue, and behaviors.)

5. Choose an adjective to describe a character in a story you've read. Find three examples from the story to support your opinion based on dialogue and action, not on descriptions by the author. Write a paragraph using the adjective in the topic sentence and your examples in supporting sentences.

6. Discuss or list a series of behaviors by one of the main characters in a story. Describe the character's values based on those actions.

7. If there is a change in a character, explain why.

8. Using a pile of headlines and a pile of news articles, match the headlines to the articles.

   Note: the teacher will have to cut these out and separate the headlines and the articles first, or friends can do this for each other.

9. After reading a story, write or tell the main idea, giving details from the story to support your answer.

10. Cover the moral of a fable. Read the fable and decide what the moral should be. Uncover the moral to find out if you were right. (Grades 4-8)

11. Explain the meaning of the moral of a fable in your own words. (Grades 4-8)

12. Find the theme in each of the following Scriptures:

    Several parables chosen from Matthew, Mark, Luke or John
    Ecclesiastes 3:1-8 (A time for everything.)
    Psalm 23 (The Lord is my Shepherd, I shall not want.)

13. As you read your Bible, look for other themes.

14. Fill in a book outline with the following information: (Grades 5-8)
    Title:
    Author:
    Purpose:
    Point of View:
    Setting:
    Main Characters:
    Plot:
    Main Idea:
    Evaluation: (An opinion supported with examples from the story.)

15. Read a biography about someone with a handicap (Helen Keller, for example). Try doing common tasks with the same handicap. Has your attitude toward handicaps changed? If so, how? Why? If not, why not?

16. After reading a story or factual information in which the conflict is based on two opposing points of view, choose a side and defend your position. (Historical fiction—cattle ranchers versus farmers, for example.)

17. Choose a position on a controversy from any historical period. Write and present your own speech or recreate a famous speech from that time.

18. Political cartoons offer a look at satire. Have the student explain the meaning of a political cartoon. If he doesn't understand it, have him look for any editorials that might help him (pointing any out, if necessary). If there are no editorials or obvious news articles to supply the necessary facts concerning what is being made fun of, explain that cartoon and select another one for the student. Interest in understanding political cartoons can spur an interest in politics and world events.

19. Have the student agree or disagree with the political cartoonist, and defend his opinion with facts.

Predict Outcomes / Make Up Reasonable Conclusions

1. Choose a problem presented in the story or article and write it clearly. Then list the facts and solution. Now write down other possible solutions. Put a star by the solution you think is the most practical. (Or discuss your ideas, instead of writing them.)

2. Listen to or read a story up to the climax (the most exciting point, and before the solution or resolution). Write your own ending.

3. Choose a character from a story set anywhere but in our present world. Write as if you are that character suddenly placed in our time and world. What would he think and say? How would people react to him? The problem of the story is "Can he adjust?" Decide how to resolve that problem and then write your story.

4. Write a fable with a moral. Remember, fables use animals that have the characteristics of people (personification) to make their point.

5. Write a short story. A short story must include characters, setting, a problem, action moving toward that problem, a climax, and an ending where the problem is resolved.

The beginning should introduce the reader to the characters and to where the story takes place. It should also give clues or hints about what is going to happen. The middle of the story should present one or more problems and tell what happens to the characters—what they do, think, and say. The ending should give a solution to the problem, answer any questions the reader may still have from reading the beginning and middle, and bring the action to a close.

Identify Facts and Opinions

1. Choose an article from the newspaper that interests you. Underline the facts. Circle the opinions. Do the facts support the opinions? If there are no opinions, write your own, using the facts as support.

2. Have the student select any news story and any editorial. Have him decide on the main difference between the two, other than the subject matter.
(News stories should be factual, unbiased accounts. Editorials offer opinions.)

3. Find movie and book reviews in newspapers and magazines.

Underline facts and circle opinions. Make one pile of reviews that convinced you to agree with the author, and one pile of those that did not convince you. Put a number on each review. Make a chart with the headings: Fact, Opinion, Convinced? Down the side, list the numbers you used to label each review.

Now fill in the number of facts and opinions you found in each review and write yes or no under Convinced? Did the review that convinced you have more of either facts or opinions than the others? Or wasn't there any pattern? If not, what did convince you? (Grades 5-8)

4. Check facts from two sources. Identify discrepancies and similarities between facts. (Grades 5-8)

Identify Techniques to Persuade:

Refer to the list of techniques described on pages 63-64.

1. Describe what a commercial or ad is declaring as important in order to convince you to buy its product. Does this fit into any specific category of propaganda techniques? If so, which category?

2. Choose an advertisement in a magazine or newspaper and list techniques used to make that product appealing.

3. Have the student look at advertisements for movies. He should select two that have pictures and quotations and tell or write what techniques are being used to persuade readers to see the film. Then have him decide what kind of audience the ad is intended to appeal to—for example, kids, families, Christians, teenagers, people that want to see violence, etc. He should support his opinions from details in the ad.

Persuasive Writing

1. Write an ad to sell an item in your home (words only). Look at ads in the classified section of the newspaper for examples.

2. Create an imaginary product and write an ad to sell it. Look at ads in magazines and on billboards for examples. Use both words and pictures.

3. Write a commercial. Sell your own imaginary product. Design a package for your product. Write a script for a TV commercial to be acted out to sell the product. What propaganda techniques (if any) will you use? (Refer to page 63.)

4. Write a critical review of a book, movie, television program, play, artwork, or selection of music. A critic is someone that makes a judgment. His opinion should help the reader decide whether or not the selection he is reviewing is worth reading, watching, purchasing, or listening to.

Before writing decide who you want to persuade (which age, social, or economic group, etc.) and what point you want to make. Then decide what information to use to make those points clear to that audience.

5. Write an interview. Choose a person you can talk to, or choose an author and answer your questions by reading about the author. Remember to list questions and answers before you write the final interview. Use questions that include who, what, when, where, why and how.

6. Choose a value or belief that you want others to agree with and write a short story that could persuade others to your value. For example: Don't lie. The story might have someone in a situation where he lies, pays a consequence and learns the lesson. Another possibility might be to have a character want to lie (and the reader would be sympathetic), but muster the courage not to. The story should include what happens because he didn't lie.

7. Write a letter to the editor opposing an issue currently under discussion in the newspaper. Include reasons supported by details and examples.

(*Comprehensive Composition* contains specific helps for teaching persuasive writing.)

STUDY SKILLS
Grades 5-8

1. Study for an oral or written test by rereading material fairly quickly and highlighting or writing down key phrases (main ideas).

2. Outline information you gather for a report. Use the outline to give an oral presentation.

Teacher Directed Activities

Library Skills (pages 73-74)

1. While at the library, have the student observe which system of cataloging books is being used. Give him a list of types of books (encyclopedia, maps, stories, biographies, poems—refer to page 74) and have him use the library's key to help him find and show you the areas for those books. *(Library Skills Grades 3-8)*

2. Have the student examine cards in the card catalog. He should eventually be able to look at any card and tell you whether it is a subject, author, or title card, and what information, and its meaning, is found on each type of card. *(Library Skills Grades 3-8) While many libraries have replaced the card catalog with computers, students should become familiar with the older filing method.*

3. Give the student a list of titles. The student tells or writes which numbers or letters define its category using the charts for the Dewey Decimal and Library of Congress Systems on page 74. *(Library Skills Grades 4-8)*

Using the Newspaper

Parts of the newspaper students should recognize are listed on page 75.

1. Ask the student to tell you what kind of information he can find in the newspaper. Notice whether or not he first looks at the index. If not, ask if there is a quicker way of answering that question. *(Study Skills Grades 7-8)*

2. Have the student select any news story and any editorial. Have him decide on the main difference between the two, other than the subject matter. *(Fact/Opinion, Using newspapers, Grades 7-8)*

   (News stories should be factual, unbiased accounts. Editorials offer opinions.)

3. Have the student look in the newspaper for movie advertisements. He should select two that have pictures and quotations and tell or write what techniques are being used to persuade readers to see the film. Then have him decide

what kind of audience the ad is intended to appeal to—kids, families, Christians, teenagers, people that want to see violence. He should support his opinions from details in the ad. *(Persuasive Techniques, Newspapers Grades 7-8)*

4. Political cartoons offer a look at satire. Provide students with political cartoons and ask students to explain the meaning of each. If he doesn't understand it, have him look for any editorials that might help him (point any out, if necessary). If there are no editorials, or obvious news articles to supply the necessary fact being made fun of, explain the cartoon. Wanting to look at and understand such cartoons can spur an interest in politics and world events. *(Inference, newspapers Grades 7-8)*

5. Ask each student to select a political cartoon and argue for or against the opinion expressed by the cartoonist. *(Draw Conclusions)*

6. Have students check several different newspapers and collect political cartoons on the same subject—both pro and con. They should then explain why they agree with one position and disagree with the other.

COMPREHENDING FICTION

Fiction refers to writing which comes from the imagination of the author, rather than writing which presents itself as factual. Tales, short stories, novels, drama, and narrative poetry (which tells a story) are all forms of fiction.

Comprehension beyond the literal meaning increases as students become aware of the various types of fiction, the elements of literature, and the various devices used in literature—figures of speech, imagery, symbolism, and so on. These aspects of literature are taught in progressively greater depth from fourth through eighth grade, but should be referred to in a natural way from first grade on.

Young children can interpret basic meaning, identify moods, differentiate between major and minor characters, recall events in a story, summarize a story, and suggest alternate solutions. In grades 4-6 most students are also able to recognize and identify various literary devices, look more deeply into character development and motivation, judge events in the plot as probable or not, and offer reasonable solutions. In grades 7-12 students are taught to not only recognize literary devices—form, elements, and use of language, but to explore the broader implications of the themes and experiences in the story, looking at them in the broader context of society.

 **TYPES OF FICTION**

Students should listen to, read, and/or watch productions of classic and contemporary literature representing a wide variety of cultures and time periods.

Skill: Identify the type of fiction based on characteristics observed within the selection heard or read.   *(See below.)*

Expectations vary. While all types of fiction are read aloud to children, or read by children, they are first taught merely to distinguish between three major forms—tales, poems, and short stories. At age nine or older, students are more able to distinguish between a variety of forms, identifying them specifically based on characteristics.

A simple teaching method is to point out the type of fiction or nonfiction being read aloud or assigned to the student, explaining why it fits that category. (Use characteristics listed here and in *Comprehending Nonfiction*.) Provide background when necessary. For example, when reading *The Odyssey* aloud discuss the time period and mention that Homer wrote this as a poem about a bigger-than-life hero. That makes it an epic poem. When students have become familiar with a few types, ask them to decide what type you have read or they are reading and give their reasons. Students old enough to maintain a personal list of books read, can include the type of fiction next to each title.

Ballad A long poem of many stanzas that tells a story and is usually sung.

Biographical Fiction A story about a real person which, while using real events, may also include imaginary conversations, thoughts, actions, and even characters.

Concrete Poem The words and the shape, or physical arrangement of the letters, are used to help convey the poem's meaning.

Epic A long, narrative poem in an elevated style that recounts the deeds of a dead hero (or heroes). The hero is of great significance historically, nationally, or in legend; the setting covers nations, the world or the universe; the action involves deeds requiring extraordinary courage or strength; and supernatural forces often involve themselves in the affairs of the hero. Example: Homer's *The Iliad*.

Fable A short tale usually using animals as human-like characters to teach a moral or lesson. Example: *Aesop's Fables*.

Fairy Tale Stories containing spirit-beings with specific qualities that are drawn on throughout the adventure. Example: *Cinderella*
These were an entertaining way of teaching virtues like kindness and courage—qualities which are rewarded only after difficulties have been faced.

Fantasy A story that takes place in a nonexistent and unreal world, like fairyland or another planet, and/or concerns unreal characters. Although it often uses magic, there is a logic consistent with the universe in which the story takes place. Example: *The Chronicles of Narnia* by C.S. Lewis

Folklore Traditional tales and beliefs of a people originally passed down through generations orally, rather than in written form. Folk means "people," lore means "doctrine (belief)" or "learning." It includes myths, legends, stories, rhymes, proverbs, riddles, songs, and more.

Folktale Stories of a people that were originally passed down orally, often containing customs, traditions, beliefs, and magic. They are concerned with objective and understandable themes such as earning a living, escaping from powerful enemies, or accomplishing difficult tasks. Characters tend to be all good or all bad.

Free Verse Poetry that uses irregular rhythm (meter) and rhyme.

Haiku A Japanese lyric poem arranged in three lines of 5, 7, and 5 syllables. The lines do not need to rhyme. Haikus generally express feelings and observations about nature.

Historical Fiction A mixture of real history and fiction. The setting and historical events are real. Actual persons from the period are often mentioned or are characters in the story. Fictitious persons are also included, and are often the main characters. Example: *Johnny Tremain* by Esther Forbes.

Humor Any work whose main intent is to amuse (although serious issues may be dealt with as in *The Adventures of Huckleberry Finn* by Mark Twain)

Legend A story or tradition handed down from the past which may be based, in part, on historical characters, places and events. (For example, King Arthur was probably a real fifth or sixth century Celtic chieftain whose exploits became exaggerated over time.) Legends tend to rely less on gods and magic than do myths.

Limerick A silly, humorous verse of five lines that has a fixed rhyme and meter. Lines 1, 2, and 5 rhyme with each other, as do lines 3 and 4.

Lyric Poem Poem expressing the strong emotions and thoughts of the author.

Mystery A story centered around the solving of some mysterious crime, or dealing with the threat of violence or illegal actions. It includes suspense, clues and important details. The problem is identified early and clues are given from time to time so that the reader may become involved with the main character(s) in solving the crime.

Myths
Ancient stories usually centering around pagan gods which attempt to explain the creation, deity, man's role, the purpose of life, death, and how things in nature came to be—the sun, moon, stars, rain, earthquakes, volcanoes, and so on.

Narrative
Written, fictionalized account of an event or series of events.

Narrative Poem
A poem which tells a story (including epics and ballads).

Novel
A book-length work of fiction.

Parable
A short story which illustrates a moral or a religious principle.

Parody
A humorous imitation meant to make fun of another author's work. (Grades 7-12)

Play
The dramatic presentation of a story. Actors portray the characters on a stage which is "dressed" to represent the setting of the action. Some plays contain a narrator, a character who talks to the audience in order to give information not presented in the dialogue. Students reading plays will notice that characters and setting are listed and stage directions and directions to actors are written in parenthesis.

Poem (Poetry)
Poetry comes in many forms and may be defined differently by many people (especially during various periods of time). However, in general, it is a composition in verse that attempts to express universal truths by stimulating emotion, and creating sensory impressions through vivid language (especially figures of speech). Poems are rhythmical and orderly in structure and often contain lines whose end words rhyme. (NOTE: The best way to begin understanding what poetry is is to read lots of it.)

Realistic Fiction
A story about people and/or events that could exist or occur.

Riddle
A clever or humorous question posed as a problem to be solved, usually asked in such a way as to be mystifying or even misleading.

Science Fiction
A form of fantasy in which scientific facts or projections form the basis of the adventure. It often takes place in the future, on other planets, or in other dimensions. Example: *C.S. Lewis' Perelandra*.

Short Story
A story shorter than a novel, but with a theme that is fully developed.

Tall Tale   An uncomplicated, humorous story that uses realistic detail and speech to tell wildly exaggerated or impossible happenings as if they are real. These incredible feats are usually accomplished by the main character, who has superhuman abilities. The purpose is to entertain. Example: Tales about Paul Bunyan and Pecos Bill.

STORY ELEMENTS

characters, setting, plot, theme

Skills:

❑   Identify elements in a story and in a play by naming characters (including the narrator), describing the setting (and scene) and plot, and restating the main idea.

❑   Differentiate between fact and fantasy, fact and opinion, and fiction and nonfiction.

❑   Identify the author's purpose: to entertain, inform, or persuade (or a combination of all three).

❑   Infer emotions or mood of a character.

❑   Infer personality traits of characters, locating evidence within the selection for support.

❑   Describe the development of a character in a fictional work.

❑   Infer the setting in a story (if not specified).

❑   Analyze the plot by describing who acted, what action(s) was taken, and the result of that action(s).

❑   Offer other reasonable conclusions to a story.

❑   Indicate recall of what was read or heard by restating information or story events in a logical order orally or in writing.

❑   Indicate comprehension of the main idea of a selection by explaining it succinctly.

❑   Identify the tone of a poem or story, explaining how it was achieved by referring to various uses of language, including archaic, formal and/or informal, dialect, figures of speech, and any relevant story elements (e.g. character, setting, and plot devices).

CHARACTERS   **People or animals in a story.**

    Ask   Who are they?
                 How are they revealed?
                 Do they change? For the better?
                 What caused them to change?

Development of a character is usually presented in one of three ways:

1. By direct statements by the author, which are then illustrated by actions.

2. Directly through the thoughts and feelings of the character without any other statements by the author, leaving the reader to infer any character traits.

3. By actions and reactions, and conversations of the character throughout the story, rather than any statements by the author. Again, traits are to be inferred.

Well-developed characters have both strengths and weaknesses, they are not all good or all bad, and their actions are consistent with their personalities. While the reader may not like a character, he should come to understand him.

SETTING   **The time(s) and place(s) in which the actions occur.**

    Ask   Where and when does the story take place?

PLOT   **The problem to be solved, events leading up to it, and its solution.**

    Ask   What happens in the story?

Plot refers to a series of events or actions that tell the reader what is happening, to whom and why. All of these events revolve around a major conflict or problem.

The **storyline** is a listing of all the events in a story from beginning to end. It tells who the story is about and what happens, but not why it happens.

Plots usually follow a basic pattern:

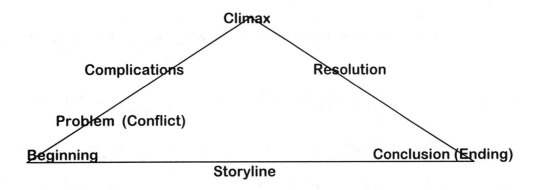

The **beginning** reveals the setting and characters, and background information that the reader will need to understand the plot.

The **middle** develops the problem or **conflict**. Two opposing forces struggle over something. That "something" becomes the problem to be overcome. Most stories involve several problems, but lead up to one major conflict—the most exciting part. This portion is also called the *rising action*.

The peak or **climax** of the story is also the **turning point**. That is—all the action has lead up to this point, and the reader is now the most emotionally involved. The story then turns toward the solution, or **resolution**. All the complications of the plot are now untangled or resolved. This portion is called the **denouncement** or **falling action**.

The ending, or **conclusion**, sometimes sums up the theme. If the plot is well-developed, the reader will find the solution to each problem believable. If the ending offers the reader a sense of hope for the future, even if it is also sad, the reader will feel satisfied.

Types of Conflict (two opposing forces struggling against each other):

- **Man against man**: One character against another.

- **Man against society**: One character against the accepted ways of behaving or thinking.

- **Man against himself**: A struggle within the character. Usually the character is faced with a difficult decision or choice.

- **Man against nature**: A character struggles against the forces of nature.

- **Man against the unknown**: A character struggles against something he can't comprehend—magic, death, a supernatural force.

THEME   The underlying message or purpose of the story.

Ask   What is the main idea? What is the author trying to say?

Ask young children: What lesson does the author want us to learn?

The theme can appear as a direct statement or, more often, must be inferred. Look for an observation or lesson by the author about life and life's experiences.

In short children's stories, the theme may be stated as part of the dialogue between characters. Point these out to the very young. As children mature, direct them to any direct statements. Otherwise, direct them to the clues that allow the reader to infer the theme. Longer works may include a statement by the author near the beginning and/or end of the novel, or provide a summary of points that allow the reader to infer the theme.

Examples of themes:

- Friends should encourage each other.
- Don't lie even if it's because you don't want to hurt someone's feelings.
- Words spoken carelessly can be harmful.
- It's okay to feel sad.
- Time passes quickly.

THE LANGUAGE OF LITERATURE

Skills:

❑ Identify the point of view of the story (first or third person).

❑ Develop an understanding of imagery produced through the use of vivid description and figurative language. Students should be able to explain both the literal and non-literal meanings of idioms, similes, metaphors, etc.

❑ Explain how the author's choice of vocabulary contributes to a story.

❑ Identify the tone of a poem or story, explaining how that was achieved by referring to various uses of language including archaic, formal and informal language and use of dialect, figures of speech, and any relevant story elements (e.g., character, setting, plot devices).

POINT OF VIEW   From whose vantage point the story is told.
(Not to be confused with the actual opinion of the author.)

Ask   Who tells the story? (Who is the narrator?)

First person   Someone in the story tells the story as he experienced it. (The "I" point of view).

Third person   Like the omniscient narrator (below), the third person (limited) tells a story about others (the "them" point of view). However, he is restricted to what he sees and hears and cannot know what others are thinking or what is happening elsewhere.

Omniscient point of view* A third person narrator who knows-all and is not restricted by time, place or character in moving or commenting. He can tell you what anyone is thinking or feeling, and what is happening in other places at the same time.

*Students are not usually asked to distinguish between the omniscient and limited third person point of view until junior high or high school.

STYLE   **The combination of the individuality of the author and how his ideas are expressed.**

By reading (or hearing) several works by one author and then several by another, a child begins to develop a sense of the uniqueness of style—much like recognizing an artist just by looking at a painting.

TONE   **1) The mood of the story.**

2) The attitude toward the subject and the audience.

Language Used to Help Create Mood

Alliteration   The beginning consonant sounds of several words or syllables in a row are all the same: *six simple songs sung softly* (Grades 2-8)

Imagery   Figures of speech, vivid description, or sensory words used to create an image.

Sensory Words   Words appealing to the senses—sight, sound, smell, taste, touch.

Symbolism   An object, character, or action that stands for something else.

Language That Shows Attitude

Formal Language   A serious, dignified use of language, avoiding slang.

Humor   Writing meant to elicit amusement. It may use contrast, sarcasm, exaggeration, repetition, puns, etc.

Informal Language   A conversational, easy manner conveyed through the use of everyday language.

Irony   Tongue-in-cheek writing which conveys the opposite meaning of what is being said. For example, calling a tall man "Shorty." (Situations which are ironic are described in *Figurative Language*.)

Sarcasm   A form of irony in which the disapproval is especially personal, obvious, and biting.

Satire   Ridicule that also uses humor and wit with the purpose of bringing about social change.

Figurative Language

Makes use of figures of speech:

Hyperbole   Exaggeration for effect. *I must have washed a million dishes.*

Idiom   An expression that means something different then what the individual words actually mean. *Jenny kept an eye on the baby.*

Irony   In a situation, what happens is the opposite of what is expected. In speech, what is said is the opposite of what is meant.

Jargon   A specialized vocabulary used by a group of people (legal jargon), or confused speech.

Metaphor   A metaphor presents (or implicitly compares) one thing as if it were another unlike thing. For example: *nerves of steel, bridle your anger, drowning in money.*

Onomatopoeia   A word whose sound suggests its meaning. For example, buzz, splash, hiss, tick-tock. (Grades 2-8)

Personification   Giving an object, animal, or idea the qualities of a person—thought and emotions. *The sea wailed and moaned.*

Simile   A direct comparison of two basically unlike things using the words *like* or *as*. *The boy was as quiet as a mouse.*

More Uses of Language

Archaic Language   Words and expressions used in the past (old-fashioned language). It is used to help place a story in a setting, making the characters a part of the time period.

Connotation   Feelings and ideas suggested by a word.

Denotation   The dictionary definition of a word.

Dialect   A difference in the way of speaking—vocabulary and pronunciation, by a specific group of people or in a specific area.

Exaggeration   Overstatement used deliberately for emphasis or humor. (Used in tall tales like *Pecos Bill*.)

Palindrome   A word, verse, or sentence that reads the same backwards as forwards. *Madam, I'm Adam.*

Precise Language   Using exact words in a description.

Pun   A humorous play on words using words with similar sounds, but different meanings. For example, the statement "Death is a grave matter!" plays on two meanings of the word grave. Grave means "serious" or "somber," which death certainly is. But a grave is also where the dead are buried. Puns are also used in riddles: *What's black and white and read (red) all over? — A newspaper.*

Writing Techniques   Grades 5 - 8

Analogy   A form of inference that assumes that because two things are alike in certain respects they are probably alike in others. Conclusions are then often formed about the former based on the latter. It is frequently used to introduce an unfamiliar concept by relating certain of its points to those of a more familiar concept.

Dialogue   Conversation between characters. It not only helps tell the story, but can reveal what those characters are like.

Foreshadowing   Hints of something that will happen in the future. Used to build interest. *(A seemingly unimportant conversation about whether or not the car needs gas could hint at a later complication caused by running out of gasoline.)*

Flashback   Interrupting the action in order to present something that happened in the past.

Narrative   How the sequence of events in an author's work is told. Description by the writer to give information, create a scene, or to present the narrator's point of view all come into play. For example, some stories are enhanced by the technique of a first person narrator; others are more effective when the narrator is omniscient.

Repetition   Repeating key words or phrases to create an atmosphere of fear, suspense, mystery, excitement, or humor. It is also used for emphasis.

Recognizing techniques used by an author, and how they enhance a story, helps a reader become a better writer. He begins to realize that it takes a combination of techniques to keep a story from becoming boring.

HIGH SCHOOL

At the high school level recognition of all of these points are practiced as part of an in-depth examination of literature. At least one work of satire should be included. Uses of language, style, tone and other points listed should be discussed.

COMPREHENDING NONFICTION

Nonfiction refers to factual writing about actual events, people, or things.

 Nonfiction writing is found in newspapers, articles, textbooks, and books covering innumerable topics. When reading nonfiction, watch for bias or statements of facts that are based on ideas that new information may now prove wrong.

Skills:

❑   Differentiate between fact and fantasy, fact and opinion, and fiction and nonfiction.

❑   Identify the author's purpose: to entertain, inform, or persuade.

❑   Draw conclusions—make generalizations based on the selection read or heard.

❑   Recognize a variety of persuasive and propaganda techniques and ways in which they are used.

❑   Evaluate material for propaganda and bias.

❑   Evaluate information and provide evidence to support your opinion.

 ## TYPES OF NONFICTION

Autobiography   A person's own account of his or her life.

Biography   A factual account of a real person's life written by someone else.

Expository Writing   Writing that explains or describes.

Informational Article   The <u>primary</u> purpose of the article is not to persuade you about something regarding a subject, but to inform you about that subject.

Narrative   A factual account of events or a series of events.

Personal Narrative   An episode in the author's life.

TECHNIQUES TO PERSUADE

Advertisements on television and in magazines and newspapers can be used for discussion of propaganda techniques. When young children beg for something advertised, informally discuss how the commercial tries to convince them to buy it.

ASSUMPTIONS

Statements made without proof that the reader is expected to take for granted as true. They may or may not be true.

BIAS

Carefully selecting facts to present a view that the author believes (for or against something), and ignoring any facts to the contrary.

Clues

Emotional words, phrases, and opinions. Statements made as fact that are actually assumptions (assumed to be true, not proven).

PROPAGANDA

A deliberate attempt to persuade in favor of, or against, someone or something. Propaganda may use one or a combination of the following techniques:

Bandwagon

Because others agree (for or against) or do such-and-such, so should you.

Compare and Contrast

Without proof, one product is compared to another as being superior.

Emotional Words

Choosing words that will arouse emotions rather than give real information.

Faulty Cause and Effect

Without proof one thing is presented as if it caused another. Statistics are often used this way, stating something has increased since something else has increased or decreased, even though what caused those rises and falls is completely unrelated.

Name-Calling

Use of <u>unsupported</u> accusations to discredit someone or something.

Repetition	Repeating a word, phrase, or slogan so that it "sticks" in the reader's or hearer's mind.
Strawman	Accusing an individual (or group) of holding an unpopular position he does <u>not</u> hold, and then arguing against that position. (Variation of name-calling.)
Testimonial	The endorsement of a person, a cause, or a product— frequently by a famous person or group.
Transfer	Shows a person with admirable qualities together with the object or person being presented so that you will associate the two and, wanting to be like the one you admire, will want the object or will support the person.

 **EVALUATING WHAT YOU READ**

1. Identify **facts** and **opinions**. (Grades 3 - 8)

    Facts can be checked and proven by using other sources of information.

    Opinions are the ideas of the author (or others he agrees with).

    *   The use of *"probably,"* or *"I think"* indicates an opinion.

    *   Because opinions are often stated as if they are facts, one must read carefully.

    *   Facts may be mixed in with opinions in order to confuse the reader into believing everything presented is a fact.

2. Evaluate the **sources** of information. (Grades 6-8)

    *   Determine which reference source is appropriate for the type of information needed.

- Consider copyright date when reading statements of fact. Scientists are continually experimenting and learning, which changes ideas that are considered proven facts. (For example, it was a well-known scientific "fact" 100 years ago that man would never fly in a heavier-than-air vehicle.)

- Check the qualifications of the author. Is he an expert in field about which he is writing or giving an opinion? If so, you may choose to agree with his ideas, or give merit to his interpretation of facts. However, if he is writing about a subject outside his field of expertise, he is no more qualified than any other ordinary person. For example, you may agree with an actor's statements about skills involved in acting, but that does not make him an expert on environmental issues.

3. Distinguish between opinion, bias, assumption, propaganda techniques, and reliable facts.

STUDY SKILLS

Skill:

❑ Use clues from pictures, diagrams, titles, headings, and context to understand meaning.

❑ Develop the habit of using a dictionary, glossary, or thesaurus in order to find out the meaning of a word. (Ability to alphabetize is necessary to do this efficiently).

❑ Learn to read information from charts, graphs, diagrams, maps, and globes.

❑ Locate books in a library using the card catalog (or computer), including reference books.

❑ Find information in a variety of reference materials: E.g., atlas, dictionary, encyclopedia, globe, newspaper, telephone directory, and thesaurus.

❑ Locate information quickly: skim or scan material, use the table of contents, index, and/or glossary.

❑ Adjust reading rate to suit the purpose.

❑ Answer questions by locating information in a selection.

❑ Take notes and organize them for study.

 ## LOCATING INFORMATION WITHIN BOOKS

Locating information with books requires knowledge of the parts of a book, as well as the ability to interpret information. Skills are listed next to the grade in which they are introduced. Practice of those skills continues throughout later grades.

Kindergarten	Identify the title.
Grade 1	Alphabetize. Use a table of contents.
Grade 2	Skim to find answers to questions in information already read.
Grade 3	Use an index and glossary Interpret information from charts, diagrams, graphs, schedules, tables, and timelines.
Grade 4	Use guide words to locate information Adjust reading speed to suit purpose: skim, scan, survey, study.

Grade 6	Use appendix, glossary, bibliography.
Grade 7	Use appendices, footnotes, and information from the title page: copyright, title, publishing company, city of publication.
Grade 8	Identify information available in the preface and acknowledgments.

Alphabetical Order

This skill is basic to using all reference materials. Teach alphabetizing by the first letter only, then by the first two letters, the first three, and so on. If a title begins with *A*, *An*, or *The*, alphabetize according to the second word in the title. Practice can be included in other studies—alphabetizing the weekly list of spelling words or searching for a book in the card catalog during a trip to the library, for example.

Reading Speed

In order to locate information quickly, a student should be able to adjust his speed and purpose, demonstrating an ability to skim, scan, and survey using headings, as well as going over material to study it. Although children learn to read quickly (skim) to find answers in grades 2 and 3, practice adjusting rate to a specific purpose does not begin until grade 4. Then it should be taught in a practical context as the student needs the skill. Studying and surveying material may be delayed until grades 6 or 7 since the SQRRR study method is not introduced until grade 6 or later.

Skim

Read material quickly and lightly to locate bits of information. Beginning in second grade, have students use this to find answers to questions in material they have already read. Skimming is also used to find information to prove a point.

Scan

Read faster than normal, but more slowly than when skimming. Read from point to point to find specific, literal information. That is, read titles, headings, and the first two or three sentences of a paragraph to decide whether the information you are looking for is likely to be in that paragraph.

Survey

Read fairly quickly in order to get an overview. It can be a point-to-point search, or a more careful look to decide on the nature of the work and to judge it. It is looking at the whole work, rather than for isolated information that sets it apart from skimming and scanning.

Study

Read and then reread with the purpose of passing judgment. Details must be noticed as support of main ideas. Evaluation skills are involved, rather than simply picking out the sentence or paragraph that answers a question, as in skimming and scanning.

SQRRR STUDY METHOD
Survey-Question-Read-Review-Recall

The SQRRR ("S-Q-3R") method can be practiced with subject textbooks in preparation for a test. It should be practiced in high school in preparation for college classes.
Grades 6-12

Survey   (Look over): Read the title, instructions, headings, words in a different type, summary points or conclusions, and captions under pictures. Look at the pictures. (Get an overview)

Question   Starting with one section, look again at the headings and subheadings and use them to think of questions to find the answer to. Ask questions that allow you to get more understanding than one or two words could answer. You can turn the headings into questions, or use the "5 W's" and "H" as your guide (who, what, when, where, why, and how).

Read   Read the material with your questions in mind. When you find an answer, stop and think about it, write a word or phrase in your notebook to help you remember it.

Recite   When you have finished a section, stop and recite it in your own words (to yourself). By putting it into your own words, you will be able to decide what you do and don't understand, and what you may need to find out more about. Now it will be easier to remember what you have read. Continue using Question-Read-Recite throughout the material.

Review   Once you have finished a section, go back over the headings and try to remember the answers you discovered. Tell yourself the main idea and the details that support it in each section. Use your notes to help you remember. Do this review after you finish the reading, and again every few days if it is information you need to remember for a test.

USING REFERENCE BOOKS

Specialized information is available in reference materials. Children need to know what kind of information is given in each source in order to decide quickly where to find information they need. Allow students to spend time with various reference books in order to determine what each contains. Then provide opportunities for practical use of references—looking for answers to questions, preparing presentations or reports, or to check the accuracy of information. This, rather than merely completing workbook pages, will ensure that the students become capable of learning independently.

The chart below provides a general idea of when specific references are frequently introduced. They are then used regularly in the grades that follow.

Grade 2   Dictionary
           Encyclopedia

Grade 3   Charts, Diagrams, Bar graphs, Pictographs
           Globe
           Within a book: glossary, index

Grade 4   Telephone Directory (including yellow pages)
           Card catalog
           Maps
           Timelines

Grade 5   Line graphs, Circle graphs

Grade 6   Atlas
           Almanac
           Computer

Grade 7   Newspaper
           Periodicals
           Within a book: appendices, footnotes, bibliography
           Within a dictionary: geographic and biographical entries, tables of weights and
               measures, and various lists: abbreviations, colleges and universities, proofreading
               marks.

ALMANAC   Short descriptions, statistics, famous dates, notable people, list of significant things, etc. Published each year. Use for answers that require updated information. Grades 6-8

APPENDIX   Supplementary material at the end of a writing. Grade 8

ATLAS   A book of maps. See "Maps" for specific skills. Grades 6-8

BIBLIOGRAPHY   A list of sources referred to by a writer. These should be looked at as sources of further information when writing an in-depth report. Grades 7-8

CHARTS and   Become aware of parts and uses. Charts and diagrams are easily
DIAGRAMS   incorporated into science and math studies and can be explained as needed. Grades 3-8

Captions   Give the topic of the drawing. Check the accompanying text if there is not a caption.

Labels   Identify specific parts.

Use   To make difficult writing easier to understand.

COMPUTER   As a source of information: become familiar with the types of information stored in a computer database and the fact that information can be accessed from one computer to another. Some libraries use this to check other libraries for a requested book. Grades 6-8

DICTIONARY   *Natural Speller* includes activity ideas to develop dictionary skills while learning assigned spelling words.

Abbreviations as entries. Grades 5-8

Entry words: Those words followed by a definition. They are sometimes written with dots or spaces separating each syllable.

Etymology: The history of a word. When available, it is listed along with the meaning of a word. Grades 6-8

Finding unknown spellings requires looking under possible spellings of a sound. Grades 6-8

Guide words: The two words at the top of each page. The word on the left is the same as the first entry word on the page. The guide word on the right is the same as the last entry word of the page. They are to be used to quickly determine whether or not a specific word could be found on that page.

Homographs: Words spelled alike, but with different meanings, are usually listed separately. Grades 3-8

DICTIONARY

Meanings of words: Each meaning is assigned a number and often has an example sentence using the word.

Parts of Speech: Use the dictionary to identify the part of speech of a word (noun, verb, adjective, etc.). Grades 4-8

Prefixes and Suffixes as entries: Grades 5-8

Pronunciation: Use of the key at the beginning of the dictionary to find out how the sounds for consonants, vowels, and schwa (looks like an upside down "e") are represented in the phonetic respellings next to each entry word. Grades 4-8

Stress Marks: Pronounce words by using the mark indicating stress on a particular syllable. Stress may also be indicated by a syllable printed in bold lettering. Grade 3-8

Grades 7-8: Examine and make use of **information contained in the back of dictionaries**. This information varies, so students should look at a variety of dictionaries. Information may include: geographic and biographical entries, tables of weights and measures, and various lists: abbreviations, colleges and universities, proofreading marks, and so on.

ENCYCLOPEDIA

A set of books used to find in-depth information on a subject. Guide letters and volume numbers on the spine are in alphabetical and numerical order so that the appropriate volume can be chosen quickly. Grades 4-8

Index

One volume, labeled "index," can be used to look up the main topic (key word) to find out which volumes and pages contain information about a particular subject. Within each volume, long articles are divided into sections with headings. At the end of the articles there may be cross-references to other articles within the set.

GLOBE

A spherical model of the earth. Students should note the differences between globes and maps found in an atlas. Grades 3-7

GLOSSARY

A dictionary-type guide found in the back of books. Grades 3-8

GRAPHS	Used to present approximate, quantitative information in an easy-to-understand format.

    Bar Graph	Vertical or horizontal bars of various lengths; used to show quantities. Grades 3-8

    Circle Graph	Also called "pie" graph. A circle is divided into labeled parts which are percentages of a whole. Grades 5-8

    Line Graph	One or more lines, vertical or horizontal, are used to show quantitative relationships between different things. A key is necessary if more than one line is used. Grades 5-8

    Pictograph	Quantities or facts are represented by pictures or symbols and a key explains their meanings. Grades 2-3

    Timeline	Regular intervals of time marked in sequence with dates in which important names and/or a brief title to indicate noteworthy events are organized chronologically. Grades 4-8

INDEX	Grades 3-8

    Alphabetical Order	By first word in a main topic. These words are in bold type. People are listed last name first.

    Cross-references	Uses "See" or "See Also" and lists other topics that may have more information on the subject.

    Illustrations	Are indicated by letters after a page number which stands for a type of illustration: (c) chart, (d) diagram, (m) map, (p) picture.

    Key words	The index lists main topics by key words. In looking up a topic, alternative key words may need to be tried before finding a reference.

    Newspapers	Using the index to find information in a newspaper is generally taught in grades 7-8.

LIBRARY   Grades 4-8

Areas   Books, reference, periodicals, microform.

Books   Fiction, nonfiction.

Fiction   These books are in a separate section and are arranged alphabetically by the author's last name. The first two letters of the author's last names are on the spine along with the call number.

Nonfiction   These books are in a separate section and are grouped by subject. They are arranged in numerical order by call number. These call numbers identify the general subject. There is a key posted in the library, but some texts and tests require their memorization.

Call Numbers   Numbers on the spine of the book and on each of the book's two or three cards filed in the card catalog. A key posted in the library indicates their locations.

Card Catalog   An alphabetical file containing two or three cards for each book: one by author's last name, one by title, and, for some, one by subject. Title cards begin with the second word if the first word is *A*, *An*, or *The*. Each card includes the book title, author, call number, copyright date, and a brief description. Grade 3-8

Microform   Microform and microfiche of old newspapers and magazines, books, etc. All can be viewed through special machines at the library. They may have a separate card catalog.

Periodicals   Current newspapers, magazines.

Reader's Guide to Periodical Literature
                   This is an alphabetical index by subject and author that is used to find articles printed in magazines on a variety of topics.

References   Encyclopedias, dictionaries, atlases, almanacs, etc.

Systems of Classification
                   The Dewey Decimal System and Library of Congress System are most frequently taught.

LIBRARY

DEWEY DECIMAL SYSTEM

000-099	General Works	Reference sources
100-199	Philosophy	Works of thinkers (*E.g., Plato*)
200-299	Religion	Includes mythology
300-399	Sociology	Behavior of groups of people
400-499	Language	Includes foreign language
500-599	Natural Science	Astronomy, biology, etc.
600-699	Technology	How things work
700-799	Fine arts	Sculpture, painting, ballet
800-899	Literature	This does not include all novels
900-999	History	
92 or B	Biography	

LIBRARY OF CONGRESS SYSTEM

A	General Works
B	Philosophy, Psychology, Religion
C to F ...	History
G	Geography, Anthropology, Recreation
H	Social Sciences
J	Political Science
K	Law
L	Education
M	Music
N	Fine Arts
Q	Science
R	Medicine
S	Agriculture
T	Technology
U	Military Science
V	Naval Science
Z	Library Science, Bibliography

MAGAZINES   To be used as a source of information by referring to the *Reader's Guide to Periodical Literature*. Grades 7-12

MAPS   Types: physical, picture, product, road and street, topographical. Identify the characteristics of different types of maps. Grades 2-8

Symbols   Used to represent various things on a map.

Legend	Explains the meaning of the symbols. (Key)
Scale	Most maps are drawn to scale — an inch may represent a specific number of miles. The scale is used to figure out the distance between two points.

NEWSPAPER   Grades 7-8

Columns	Most newspapers have opinion columns written regularly by a specific writer.
Index	Lists major sections and regular features.
Major sections	Articles in a section relate to the topic of that section—sports, news, entertainment, and so on.
Regular features	Items in every issue, such as movie listings, television and radio schedules, and editorials.
Storage	Old newspapers are often reproduced onto microfilm and kept in libraries for viewing.

TABLES OR SCHEDULES

A way of displaying a summary of related information that is quantitative or statistical. Explanations are given by the use of captions, column headings, sideheads, and keys.

Bus, train, or airline schedules are useful for practice in reading timetables. Grades 5-7

TELEPHONE DIRECTORY

An alphabetical listing of people and services available in a city.

Children should become familiar with the various sections of the phone book, and practice using key words in order to find information. For example, where would they look to find someone to fix a clogged drain? Which section would they look in—white, yellow, or blue pages? Grades 4-8

The phone book also contains calendars to find the day of any date from 1800 to 2050. Grades 6-8

THESAURUS   A dictionary of synonyms. Useful in writing to find the most precise word, and in expanding vocabulary. Grades 4-8

COMPREHENSION SKILLS ORGANIZED BY GRADE

The grade range indicates periods in which skills are developed, not mastered.

KINDERGARTEN – GRADE 2

Immerse children in a language-rich environment. Read aloud from a wide variety of fiction and nonfiction in order to develop their vocabularies as well as their appreciation of literature even after introducing phonic instruction.

GRADE   ORAL LANGUAGE

The student will:

K-2	Identify sounds as same or different.
K-2	Identify a variety of sounds common to the child's environment.
K-2	Identify mood by tone of voice.
K-2	Follow one-, two-, three-, and four-step oral directions.
K-2	Listen to a variety of types of stories, poems, and nonfiction.
K-2	Ask and answer questions about what was heard (or read).
K-2	Ask the meaning of a word or phrase not understood.
K-2	Use words to describe size, color, shape, location.
K-2	Use words to describe people, places, things, and actions.
K-2	Identify and use synonyms and antonyms.
K-2	Identify rhyming words and pictures.
K-2	Repeat sound patterns.
K-2	Create rhyming words orally.
K-2	Differentiate between literal and non-literal meanings of figures of speech: idioms, hyperbole, personification, similes and metaphors.

READING/LITERATURE

The student will:

K-2	Distinguish between fact and fantasy.
2	Identify a selection as fiction or nonfiction.
K-2	Use pictures to make predictions about the content of a story.
K-2	Identify the emotion or mood in an illustration.
K-2	Retell short stories in sequence—beginning, middle, end.
K-2	Describe characters, settings, and events in stories and poems.
K-2	Explain the problem (conflict) of a story and how it is resolved.
K-2	Identify the main idea of a story.
K-2	Ask how and why questions about the story.
K-2	Answer who, what, when, where questions about the selection.
K-2	Interpret meaning by using inference—what is implied, not stated: Personality traits of characters. Mood (emotions) of characters.
2	Identify the elements of a play: scene, narrator, actor, actress, and its story elements: plot, characters, setting, main idea or theme.

To comprehend both fiction and nonfiction, the student will:

K-2   Distinguish between fact and fantasy.

K-2   Develop a purpose for reading (or listening).

K-2   Confirm or adjust his predictions as he reads.

K-2   Weigh alternatives. Give alternative solutions.

K-2   Relate his own previous experiences to the selection.

K-2   Use strategies for determining the meaning of a written word:
> Apply phonic skills.
> Use clues from pictures or diagrams.
> Use clues from context: sentence, paragraph.
> Use clues from titles or headings.
> Use a dictionary.
> Use a thesaurus.
> Reread as necessary.

K-2   Locate information in the selection in order to answer questions.

1-2   Follow one- and two-step written directions.

To develop skills in analysis the student will:

K   Arrange pictures in a correct sequence:
> The order of events in a story.
> The order of events observed in daily life.

K-1   Categorize pictures or objects according to similarities (compare) and differences (contrast).

2   Categorize pictures, objects, and/or words according to similarities and differences.

K-1   Identify the cause and the effect in a given relationship.

K-1   Draw conclusions—make generalizations based on the selection read (or heard.

STUDY SKILLS

The student will:

K-1   Hold a book correctly and learn to read left to write, top to bottom.

K-1   Identify the title of a book

K-1   Follow oral and written one- and two-step directions.

1   Alphabetize by the first letter of each word.

1-2   Alphabetize by the first and second letters of each word.

1-2   Use a table of contents

1-2   Use a picture dictionary

1-2   Locate information in a selection to answer questions.

2   Find information using pictures and charts.

2   Use an encyclopedia.

GRADES 3 – 4

Phonic skills become even more of a priority in this age range. Continue teaching phonics at the appropriate instructional level, but also have students practice reading out loud from selections at their independent reading level (words they have already learned) in order to develop fluency and expression. Students should read a variety of classic and contemporary fiction and nonfiction, but they should also continue to listen to selections and participate in discussions in order to develop comprehension skills appropriate to their age, rather than being limited by their reading level.

GRADE	ORAL LANGUAGE

The student will:

3-4	Use descriptive language.
3-4	Understand multiple meanings of words.
3-4	Identify and use synonyms and antonyms.
3-4	Understand the meaning of examples of figurative language and literary devices: idioms, similes, metaphors, hyperbole, personification, onomatopoeia, adages, proverbs, alliteration, puns, and palindromes.
3-4	Listen, ask and answer questions as part of a discussion.
3-4	Restate what has been said.
3-4	Present brief oral reports: speak clearly using specific vocabulary.
3-4	Follow four and five-step oral instructions. (E.g., games and recipes.)
3-4	Give oral directions for others to follow.

READING/LITERATURE

The student will:

3-4	Read and listen to a variety of types of fiction and nonfiction including autobiographies and biographies, fables, folktales, historical fiction, and poetry.
3-4	Identify the point of view of a story.

To comprehend both fiction and nonfiction, the student will:

3-4	Read and follow four and five-step directions.
3-4	Set a purpose for reading.
3-4	Make, confirm, or revise predictions.
3-4	Make up a reasonable conclusion to a story.
3-4	Use various strategies to understanding meaning: phonics, knowledge of homophones, knowledge of multiple meanings of a word, sentence structure, context, picture clues, glossary, dictionary, thesaurus.
3-4	Identify and understand the meaning of examples of figurative language and literary devices including : idioms, similes, metaphors, hyperbole, personification, onomatopoeia, adages, proverbs, alliteration, puns, and palindromes.

3-4	Relate previous experiences and learning to the selection.
3-4	Restate information orally or in writing.
3-4	Summarize the main idea of a selection in a single sentence.
3-4	Identify characteristics of several types of literature based on characteristics.
3-4	Identify a selection as a biography or an autobiography.

To develop skills in analysis the student will:

3-4	Identify the purpose of a work: to persuade, entertain, or inform.
3-4	Identify ways in which the author's choice of language, setting, and information contributes to the author's purpose.
3-4	Classify information according to similarities and differences.
3-4	Compare information within and between selections.
3-4	Compare and contrast characters in two different stories and biographies.
3-4	Organize information or events in chronological order.
3-4	Organize important points of a selection in any or all of the following ways: summary, graph, filling in an outline with main and secondary points.
3-4	Identify a statement as fact or opinion.
3-4	Identify the use of fact and fantasy in literature.
4	Evaluate sources of information. Express an opinion to accept or reject the information.
4	Begin to use evidence to support an opinion.
4	Relate content to real life.
4	Name an effect when given a cause. Name a cause when given an effect.

STUDY SKILLS

The student will:

3-4	Follow multi-step written directions.
3-4	Locate answers to questions in a selection already read.
3-4	Find the title, author, and illustrator of a book.
3-4	Alphabetize using the first three letters of each word.
3-4	Use guide words in reference books.
3-4	Use an index.
3-4	Use a glossary.
3-4	Use information from charts, diagrams, bar graphs, pictographs, maps and globes.
3-4	Use reference books: dictionary, encyclopedia, telephone directory—including the yellow pages, thesaurus.
3-4	Locate books in the library.
3-4	Use a card catalog.
3-4	Adjust reading rate to suit the purpose.
4	Use a strategy to study: memorize selected material.

GRADES 5-6

At this level, documents and speeches are often included in reading selections, as well as the wide variety of types of fiction, poetry, and nonfiction still assigned. Standards in many states now include the use of computers. Students in grades 5-8 use reference materials via a computer, create reports in a word processing program and learn how to find information using the Internet. Focus in comprehension shifts to the development of skills in analysis—evaluating information, drawing conclusions, and supporting opinions.

GRADE	ORAL LANGUAGE

The student will:

5-6	Make oral presentations using visual aids.
5-6	Use specific and appropriate vocabulary to communicate ideas.
5-6	Listen critically and express opinions.

READING/LITERATURE

The student will:

5-6	Read a variety of fiction, nonfiction, and poetry selections.
5-6	Identify the type of literature by its characteristics.

To comprehend both fiction and nonfiction, the student will:

5-6	Set a purpose for reading.
5-6	Make, confirm, or revise predictions based on knowledge of literary forms.
5-6	Make up a reasonable conclusion to a story.
5-6	Understand word meaning by using various strategies: knowledge of meanings of prefixes and suffixes, knowledge of homophones, knowledge of multiple meanings of a word, sentence structure, context, picture clues, glossary, dictionary, thesaurus.
5-6	Understand meaning using analogies.
5-6	Identify and understand the meaning of examples of figurative language and literary devices including : idioms, similes, metaphors, hyperbole, personification, onomatopoeia, jargon, irony, adages, proverbs, alliteration, puns, palindromes, dialect, and acronyms.
5-6	Relate previous experiences and learning to the selection.
5-6	Restate information orally or in writing.
5-6	Summarize the main idea of a selection in a single sentence.
5-6	Choose or create a title for a selection which reflects the main idea.

To develop skills in analysis the student will:

5-6	Identify the purpose of a work: to persuade, entertain, or inform.
5-6	Identify ways in which the author's choice of language, setting, and information contributes to the author's purpose.
5-6	Classify information according to similarities and differences.

5-6	Compare information within and between selections.
5-6	Compare and contrast characters in two different stories and biographies.
5-6	Compare and contrast styles of various authors.
5-6	Organize information or events in a logical order: chronological order, order of importance.
5-6	Organize important points of a selection in any or all of the following ways: summary, graph, filling in an outline with main and secondary points.
5-6	Identify a statement as fact or opinion.
5-6	Support opinions, predictions, and conclusions with information in the selection.
5-6	Identify cause and effect relationships.
5-6	Relate content to real life.
5-6	Describe the development of characters in fictional works.
5-6	Describe the development of the plot, explaining how conflicts are resolved.
6	Explain how the author uses the development of characters and plot to build a story's main conflict.
5-6	Explain how the author's style and choice of vocabulary enhances the selection.
6	Evaluate sources of information. Express an opinion to accept or reject the information.

STUDY SKILLS

The student will:

5-6	Use reference materials: almanac, atlas, dictionary, encyclopedia, globe, *Reader's Guide to Periodical Literature*, telephone directory, thesaurus.
5-6	Organize information to present reports.
5-6	Record information on charts, graphs, and maps.
5-6	Summarize information.
5-6	Outline material.
5-6	Skim to gain a general overview of content or to locate information.
5-6	Take notes on important content.
5-6	Find resources in the library and using a computer.
6	Use the SQRRR study method.

GRADES 7-8

Analytical skills are now applied to a bigger world—the use of media and its effects on people, the political process, the way in which literature influences or reflects a culture. Computer skills, research and study skills, and organizational skills are all developed more completely in preparation for high school. Analysis of literature includes a closer look at symbols as well as the variety of literary devices and figurative language in order to determine the effect of all these elements on the reader.

GRADE	ORAL LANGUAGE

The student will:

7-8	Listen critically and express opinions.
7-8	Give an oral presentation using both specific and appropriate vocabulary, eye contact, and appropriate gestures.
7-8	Use interviews to gain information.
7-8	Comprehend meanings of analogies, multiple word meanings, and various uses of language and literary devices.

READING/LITERATURE

The student will:

7-8	Read a variety of classic and contemporary fiction and poetry, and nonfiction which includes essays and speeches.
7-8	Identify the type of fiction or nonfiction by characteristics.
7-8	Describe the setting, plot, and theme.
7-8	Make, confirm, or revise predictions based on knowledge of literary forms.

To comprehend both fiction and nonfiction, the student will:

7-8	Set a purpose for reading.
7-8	Make, confirm, or revise predictions.
7-8	Relate previous experiences and learning to the selection.
7-8	Use knowledge of fiction and nonfiction forms to aid in comprehension.
7-8	Understand word meaning by using various strategies.
7-8	Understand meaning using analogies.
7-8	Distinguish fact from opinion in a variety of nonfiction selections, such as magazines, newspapers, and speeches.
7-8	Explain the main idea of a selection.
7-8	Summarize a selection.

To develop skills in analysis the student will:

7-8	Identify cause and effect relationships in the plot and describe their impact.
7-8	Identify themes or main ideas that are implied, not just those stated.
7-8	Explain how the author uses the development of characters and plot to support a story's main conflict.

7-8   Compare and contrast the development of literary elements (plot, character, setting, theme) in different types of fiction.

7-8   Describe how the author's choice of literary form, his style, and specifics such as point of view, tone, and word choice influences the reader.

7-8   Describe the contribution of rhythm to the purpose or theme of a poem.

7-8   Identify and explain symbols and figurative language used in a selection.

7-8   Identify persuasive techniques used in various media, distinguish between facts and opinions, identify the point or main idea.

7-8   Analyze details for accuracy and relevance to the main idea.

7-8   Examine cause-effect relationships between a work, speech, or media coverage and public opinion.

7-8   Classify, compare and contrast, and organize information for various purposes.

STUDY SKILLS

The student will:

7-8   Select and use the best sources for a specific purpose, including almanac, atlas, dictionary, encyclopedia, globe, newspaper, *Reader's Guide to Periodical Literature*, telephone directory, thesaurus.

7-8   Use appendices and bibliographies.

7-8   Find resources in the library and using a computer.

7-8   Give credit to sources used in speeches or written reports.

7-8   Use the SQRRR study method.

7-8   Organize information to present reports.

7-8   Record information on charts, graphs and maps.

COMPREHENSION SKILLS ORGANIZED BY TOPIC

Grade
Introduced   **Understanding Meaning**

K	Identify a variety of sounds common to the child's environment.
K	Identify sounds as same or different.
K	Identify mood by tone of voice.
K	Identify rhyming words and pictures.
K	Repeat sound patterns.
K	Create rhyming words orally.
K	Use words to describe size, color, shape, location, people, places, things, and actions.
K	Identify and use antonyms and synonyms.
K	Ask the meaning of a word or phrase not understood.
K	Ask how.
3	Listen, ask, and answer questions during a discussion.
3	Read aloud with expression.
3	Give brief oral presentations, speaking clearly and using specific vocabulary.
5	Give oral presentations using visual aids and specific and appropriate vocabulary.
5	Listen critically and express opinions.
7	Use interviews to gain information.
K	Use clues to find the meaning of a word: Pictures. Use in a sentence and paragraph (context).
1	Use context clues to understand the meaning of a new word: sentence, paragraph, titles, headings.
1	Reread as necessary to seek meaning.
1	Use various methods to learn word meaning: phonics, context, dictionary, thesaurus.
3	Use various strategies to understand meaning: phonics, knowledge of homophones, knowledge of multiple meanings of a word, sentence structure, context, picture clues, glossary, dictionary, thesaurus.
5	Understand meanings of analogies.
K	Differentiate between literal and non-literal meanings of figures of speech: idioms, hyperbole, personification, similes and metaphors.
3	Identify and understand the meaning of examples of figurative language and literary devices including personification, adage, and proverb.

Grade Introduced	**Understanding Meaning**
4	Identify and understand the meaning of examples of figurative language and literary devices including alliteration, puns, and palindromes.
5	Identify and understand the meaning of examples of figurative language and literary devices including dialect, and acronyms.
7	Identify and explain symbols used in literature.
K	Follow oral one- and two-step directions.
1	Follow written directions.
3	Give oral directions for others to follow.
3	Follow directions with as many as five steps.
K	Arrange pictures in a correct sequence: The order of events in a story. The order of events observed in daily life.
K	Retell short stories in sequence—beginning, middle, end.
3	Sequence: Arrange sentences in chronological order.
4	Sequence: Arrange statements in a logical sequence.
5	Sequence: Arrange statements in order of importance.
K	Develop a purpose for listening (or reading).
K	Distinguish between fact and fantasy.
2	Identify a selection as fiction or nonfiction.
3	Identify the type of fiction being read.
K	Summarize what was read by retelling the story.
4	Restate information orally or in writing.
4	Summarize the main idea of a selection in a single sentence.
5	Select or create a title that reflects the main idea.
4	Organize important points of a selection in any or all of the following ways: summary, graph, outline.
K	Identify the problem (conflict) of a story and how it is resolved.
1	Identify the story elements: plot, characters, setting, main idea, theme or moral.
2	Identify the elements of a play: scene, narrator, actor, actress, and its story elements: plot, characters, setting, main idea or theme.
3	Identify the point of view of a story.

Grade Introduced	**Thinking: Analyzing and Evaluating Information**
K	Relate content to personal experience.
3	Relate previous experiences and learning to the selection.
K	**Compare and Contrast:** Categorize pictures or objects according to similarities and differences.
2	Categorize words as well as pictures or objects.
3	Classify information according to similarities and differences.
4	Compare information within and between selections.
5	Compare the central characters in two stories.
K	Identify the **cause** and the **effect** in a given relationship.
4	Name an effect when given a cause.
	Name a cause when given an effect.
K	Identify emotion or mood in illustrations.
K	Make **predictions** about the content of a story.
K	Confirm or revise predictions as necessary.
2	Weigh alternatives. Give alternative solutions.
3	Make up a reasonable conclusion to a story.
K	Interpret meaning using **inference**—what is implied, not stated
1	**Infer** personality traits and moods of story characters.
1	**Draw conclusions**—make generalizations based on the reading.
1	Distinguish between fact and fantasy.
3	Identify the type of literature read based on its characteristics.
3	Analyze plot by describing who acted, what action(s) was taken, and what was the result(s) of that action(s).
4	Interpret the moral of a fable.
5	Interpret motive based on context and tone of what is heard or read.
6	Explain how the author uses the development of characters and plot to build a story's main conflict.
3	Identify a statement as **fact or opinion**.
3	Identify the purpose of a work: to entertain, inform, or persuade (or a combination of all three).
3	Identify the point of view of the selection: first or third person.
3	Identify the use of fact and fantasy in literature.
4	Evaluate sources of information. Express an opinion with support for accepting or rejecting given information.
5	Recognize a variety of persuasive and propaganda techniques and ways in which they are used: advertising, campaigns, newspapers, news broadcasts.

Grade Introduced	Study Skills
K	Read left to right, top to bottom.
1	Find answers to questions in material already read.
K	Identify the title.
1	Use a table of contents.
3	Find the title, author, and illustrator of a book.
1	Follow written directions.
1	Alphabetize by first letter.
2	Alphabetize by first and second letter of each word.
3	Alphabetize using the first three letters of a word.
3	Use guide words in reference books.
2	Interpret information from charts and pictures.
2	Use a dictionary and encyclopedia.
4	Use a thesaurus.
3	Use an index.
3	Use a glossary.
3	Become familiar with information available on a globe.
3	Read information from charts, diagrams, bar graphs, pictographs.
4	Find information on maps
4	Use a telephone directory, including the yellow pages.
7	Use appendices, bibliographies.
8	Use an atlas.
7	Use footnotes, information from the title page, preface, acknowledgements.
7	Use an index to find information in a newspaper.
3	Locate books in the library.
4	Use a card catalog.
5	Use the Dewey Decimal System.
7	Select and use the best sources for a specific purpose.
4	Adjust reading rate to suit the purpose.
4	Use a strategy to study.
4	Memorize selected material.
5	Outline material. (Refer to the Design-A-Study book *Comprehensive Composition*.)
6	Scan, survey, or study material as appropriate.
6	Take notes and organize them for study.
6	Use the SQRRR strategy for studying.

Grade Introduced	**Survival Skills**
K	Interpret signs.
1	Read signs.
1	Read name, address, phone number.
1	Follow directions.
3	Use a phone book, including the yellow pages.
3	Read a map.
4	Read a simple schedule *(T.V.)*.
4	Read labels, menus.
5	Understand basic first aid.
7	Understand a train or bus schedule.
7	Use a newspaper – understand classified ads.

High School level also includes:

9 - 12	Demonstrate banking skills: write a check, understand a checking account statement, understand credit vocabulary.
9 - 12	Write a resume.
9 - 12	Complete various forms including job application, and tax return.
9 - 12	Understand a driver's manual, service contracts, and an insurance policy.
9 - 12	Understand the procedure for voting.

RESOURCES

Practice materials for specific skills are available from a wide variety of companies. A few are listed below for convenience.

Anvil Press
834 Stehman Road
Millersville, PA 17551
Phone (717) 871-0617   E-mail address: lpoling@aol.com
"Engaging Young Minds Literature Guides Series." Novel guides for grades 5-12.

Cambridge Development Laboratory
86 West Street
Waltham, MA 02154
Phone 1-800-637-0047   In Massachusetts: (718) 890-4640
Language arts software.

Critical Thinking Press and Software
P.O. Box 448
Pacific Grove, CA 93950
Phone 1-800-458-4849   Fax (408) 393-3277
Web Site: www.criticalthinking.com
Workbook titles include: Dr. DooRiddles (Grades K-12), Thinkanalogy Puzzles (Grades 3-12), Critical Thinking Book 1 (Grades 7-12).

Educators Publishing Service
31 Smith Place
Cambridge, MA 02138-1000
Phone: 1-800-225-5750
Workbooks for all reading comprehension skill areas and ages, including materials suitable for children with special needs. One of the few sources providing practice with analogies.

Gamco
P.O. Box 1911
Big Spring, TX 79721-1911
Phone 1-800-351-1404   Fax 1-800-896-1760
Web Site: www.gamco.com
Software especially suited for special needs K-12, all subjects.

High Noon Books
20 Commercial Boulevard
Novato, CA 94949-6191
Phone 1-800-422-7249
Literature to interest ages 9-14 but with a reading level from first to fourth grade.

Learning Links Inc.
2300 Marcus Avenue, Dept. A92
New Hyde Park, NY 11042
Phone (516) 437-9071
Novels and study guides.

Learning Services
P. O. Box 10636
Eugene, OR 97440-2636
Phone West: 1-800-877-9378   Phone East 1-800-877-3278
Web Site: www.learnserv.com
Software for ages 4-18: Heartsoft Thinkology grades K- 4: CDs: clarity, accuracy, and logic. Queue Life Skills Compilations: Reasoning Skills grades 4-10 Reading comprehension, logic, critical thinking; Life Skills CD grades 7-12 English, reading comprehension for employment.

Novel Units
P.O. Box 791610
San Antonio, TX 78279-1610
Phone 1-800-688-3224   Fax 1-830-438-4263
Web Site: www.educyberstor.com
Novels and study guides for preK-8.

Progeny Press
200 Spring Street
Eau Claire, WI 54703-3225
Phone: (715) 833-5261 Fax: (715) 836-0105
Bible-based study guides for literature.

Total Language Plus
P.O. Box 548
Livermore, CA 94551
Phone (510) 606-5841
Novels and study guides.

J. Weston Walch, Publisher
321 Valley Street
P.O. Box 658
Portland, ME 04104-0658
Phone 1-800-341-6094 Fax (207) 772-3105
Grades 6-12 workbooks for critical thinking and reading skills (as well as other subjects) including those targeted for special needs: remedial practice, high interest but low readability materials, workplace skills.

CHECKLIST	NAME				
REASONING					
Follow oral directions					
Follow written directions					
Identify correct sequence					
Classify information alike/different					
Summarize something read					
Identify cause/effect					
Identify fact/opinion					
Predict outcome, giving reasons					
Weigh alternatives					
Give alternatives					
Identify the purpose of a work					
Identify a work as fiction or nonfiction					
Evaluate sources as to reliability					
Evaluate material for bias/propaganda					
LITERATURE *Use terms*					
Characters					
Setting					
Plot					
Conflict/problem					
Theme					
Point of view					
Tone					
Play: scene, narrator					
Infer a character's personality					
Find examples:					
Acronym					
Adage					
Alliteration					
Archaic language					
Connotation of a word					
Denotation of a word					
Dialect					
Dialogue					
Exaggeration					
Flashback					
Foreshadowing					
Formal language					
Humor					

Name:					
Idiom					
Irony – statement					
Irony – situation					
Jargon					
Metaphor					
Onomatopoeia					
Palindrome					
Personification					
Proverb					
Repetition					
Sarcasm					
Satire					
Sensory words					
Similes					
Symbolism					
Identify types of literature:					
Ballad					
Biographical fiction					
Concrete poem					
Epic					
Fable					
Fairy tale					
Fantasy					
Folklore					
Folktale					
Free verse					
Haiku					
Historical fiction					
Humor					
Legend					
Limerick					
Lyric					
Mystery					
Myth					
Narrative					
Narrative poem					
Novel					
Parable					
Parody					
Play					
Realistic fiction					
Riddle					

Name:					
Science fiction					
Short story					
Tall tale					
Autobiography					
Biography					
Expository writing					
Informational article					
Nonfiction narrative					
Reading rate: skim					
Scan					
Survey					
USE REFERENCES					
Almanac					
Library					
Magazines					
Maps					
Newspaper					
Reader's Guide to Periodical Literature					
Locate information					
Alphabetical order					
Glossary					
Index					
Table of contents					
Dictionary					
Identify entry words					
Use guide words					
Use part of speech notation					
Use pronunciation guide					
Notice other information available					
Graphs: Interpret information					
Bar graph					
Circle graph					
Line graph					
Pictograph					
Timeline					
Maps: Identify and use					
Legend					
Scale					
Symbols					

Name:					
Recognize and interpret information from:					
Picture maps					
Product maps					
Physical maps					
Topographical maps					
Road and street maps					
Library:					
Areas					
Card catalog					
Dewey Decimal System					
Library of Congress					
Microfilm resources					
Newspaper:					
Columns					
Index					
Major sections					
Regular features					
Practice **SQRRR** study technique					

HOW TO PULL IT ALL TOGETHER WITH DESIGN-A-STUDY

Design-A-Study guides provide objectives and concepts to cover, as well as tips for teaching each subject. This framework allows the teacher flexibility in meeting the student's needs. Here are just a few possibilities for customizing a curriculum:

- **Plan a history-based unit study, choosing a culture or time frame.**

1. Choose the culture or period.

2. Decide which other subjects to cover in connection with history, using the "Activity Guide" section of *Guides to History Plus.*

3. As you work in a subject, refer to the appropriate guide for the specifics of teaching that subject, and check off objectives covered.

For example: *Critical Conditioning* lists the types of books to read—nonfiction, historical fiction, fables, poems, and so on. It also lists specific reading comprehension skills, such as identifying the main idea, or drawing a conclusion. These skills can be practiced during a discussion about a story from any of the types of books in use, as well as by using supplementary workbooks. Topics for related compositions can be taken from the "Discussion Questions" in *Critical Conditioning,* or from the *Guides to History Plus'* "Question Guide" and "Activities" section. A topic in science can be chosen as it connects to the history unit. Then, *Science Scope* can provide specific objectives to be used as a guideline for that study. Students can research objectives and present an oral or written report, or the teacher can present lessons using library books, videos, kits, or other appealing resources using the Design-A-Study books as a framework .

- **List each subject to be taught, then choose objectives in those subjects from the Design-A-Study guides.**

1. Once objectives are chosen, refer to suggestions for teaching the subject in each Design-A-Study guide for insight into choosing appropriate resources. Refer to *Teaching Tips and Techniques* for help in selecting materials best suited to an individual's learning style.

2. Check off the objective in the guide once completed (date and student's initials). Remember, these guides cover several grades, allowing the student to work at his own pace. You'll find it helpful in future planning to be able to skim through the guides to note anything not covered.

Subjects can be taught individually, but still be more than artificial, isolated exercises. You may decide to teach the proper form for business letters in composition by having the student write a complimentary letter, one of complaint, or a request for information to an actual company. Subjects can also be combined at times in order to increase student interest. A literary classic set within the same time period being studied in history could be assigned (e.g., Dicken's *A Tale of Two Cities* during a study of the French Revolution) and the skills listed in *Critical Conditioning* covered through discussion and composition assignments. No matter what subject is being covered, however, it is important to find materials which appeal to the students.

- **Use a packaged curriculum, but adjust it to suit your situation using Design-A-Study guides.**

1. Check the guide in each subject area to determine the actual objectives.
   ⇒ Wait and cover those objectives later. (The grade range will indicate how long that objective is part of a curriculum.)
   ⇒ Substitute other materials to meet the same objective.
   ⇒ Skip the lesson because it has already been mastered by the student.

2. Refer to Design-A-Study guides for activity ideas to substitute for curriculum suggestions your students found unappealing.

3. Use the curriculum package for some subjects only. Replace the other subject areas with a different approach, using the packaged materials as one of several resources.
   ⇒ Check the Design-A-Study guides for objectives and teaching ideas.
   ⇒ Replace or supplement the package curriculum materials with library books or other resources that appeal to the students.

For example: Use all materials except the science text. Choose a topic from the text, but use a variety of books and projects to cover that same topic. This is an easy way to provide a refreshing change for the students, while keep planning to a minimum.

- **Allow your student's interests to dictate areas of focus, checking off objectives in the Design-A-Study guides as they are covered.**

1. The guides provide an overview that allows the teacher to cover content or skills in any order.

2. When a student has a strong area of interest which consumes much of his time, the teacher can work in objectives from other subject areas so that the student completes necessary content and skills efficiently. Anything not connected to the area of focus should be covered using methods and resources appropriate to the student's learning style.

For example: A study of history could focus on transportation, and, while including other elements listed in the question guide, could go into greater detail in this area of interest. The student could make a timeline of vehicles, read biographies of inventors, write reports on inventors and/or inventions, and write creatively about a how an invention of his own would change lives in the future. While reading related books, points in *Critical Conditioning* could be discussed. *Comprehensive Composition* could provide specifics for creative writing as well as for writing and discussing a biography. *Science Scope* could provide objectives for exploring physical science, especially machines, providing an outline for student research, or points to be covered by the teacher using any resources considered appropriate. Related word and estimation problems could be written for practice using *Maximum Math*. For example, word problems often relate to transportation: "A train leaves the station at noon, traveling at 60 m.p.h. . . ."

CHECK THE DESIGN-A-STUDY WEB SITE FOR CURRENT INFORMATION ON BOOKS AVAILABLE AND THE MONTHLY TEACHING TIPS COLUMN: http://www.designastudy.com/